MW00571757

THE BEING EQUATION

Go Create!

Erik ☺

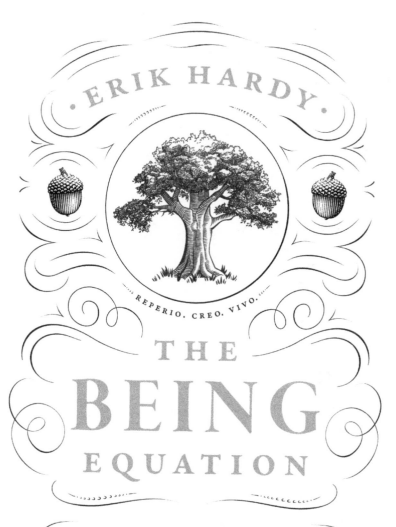

· ERIK HARDY ·

REPERIO. CREO. VIVO.

THE
BEING
EQUATION

DISCOVER WHO YOU ARE.
CREATE WHO YOU WANT TO BE.

LIONCREST
PUBLISHING

COPYRIGHT © 2021 ERIK HARDY

All rights reserved.

THE BEING EQUATION

Discover Who You Are. Create Who You Want to Be.

ISBN   978-1-5445-2267-8   *Hardcover*
       978-1-5445-2266-1   *Paperback*
       978-1-5445-2265-4   *Ebook*

To Christine—words are too small.

*To Source, my companion on the journey since
before I knew there was a journey to take.*

CONTENTS

INTRODUCTION...9

PART 1: THE EQUATION
1. START WITH WHY...13
2. THE EQUATION...17
3. SPIRIT...27
4. PHYSICAL BODY..39
5. INPUTS...53
6. LIFE EVENTS..63
7. EGOIC INTERPRETATION 85

PART 2: BEING
8. CLARITY AND KNOWLEDGE 99
9. LOVE, ACCEPTANCE, AND FORGIVENESS...........105
10. FEELINGS AND EMOTIONS.................................119
11. ENERGY..131
12. RELATIONSHIPS...137
13. MENTORS...149
14. APPLYING THE BEING EQUATION......................171

PART 3: SOLVING THE EQUATION
15. EXERCISES..187

CONCLUSION..241
ACKNOWLEDGMENTS...247
ABOUT THE AUTHOR 251

INTRODUCTION

I believe that most of our struggles in life result from a lack of clarity on the answers to two fundamental questions:

1. Who am I?
2. What am I meant to do?

I spent the first forty-two years of my life struggling with the second question: *"what am I meant to do?"* I hadn't realized that I could never answer that question until I could answer the first: *"who am I?"*

To be honest, I should say I struggled with that second question from about year fifteen through year forty-two. I do not remember worrying about what I was meant to do before I was fifteen. Before the age of fifteen, I was meant to play outside and go to school. It began getting complicated in my junior year of high school when I started applying to colleges. This process implied that I knew what I wanted to do for a career. *I had no clue.* I think most people are that way. How can you know what you are meant to do for a career when you are fifteen years old? It's insane, really, to believe that a fifteen-year-old person from a small, rural town in Virginia, with little knowledge of other countries, cultures, and people would have any real inkling of what they were meant to do for the rest of their life. Up to that point, the education system had exposed me to the basic subjects of reading, writing, and arithmetic, with a little art and music thrown in here and there. My world was *small*.

I look back at that time now and realize how little I knew and how little many of the people I relied on for advice and mentorship knew. Not out of negligence but due to a lack of their own knowledge. Having spent the past twenty years thinking about this subject—after seeing the struggles that my friends, family, and acquaintances around me had to face—I have come to realize that most people are never given any guidance as to how to answer these two fundamental questions: *who am I and what am I meant to do?*

In this book, I share what I have learned through years of reading, listening, studying, writing, and struggling with my own feelings of darkness and being lost. If what I have learned helps you and saves you some of the difficulties I faced, it will mean I am living in my greatness.

What follows is the answer to: *who am I?* which will lead you to what you are meant to do. To be fair, it is not necessarily an easy journey or a fast one, but it can be the adventure of a lifetime if you are willing to take the first step.

PART 1

THE
EQUATION

CHAPTER 1

START WITH WHY

"I never really knew what I was meant to do with my life, so I just tried to make other people happy." I can vividly remember hearing my mom casually say these words to me as we sat on her deck a few days after her seventy-fifth birthday. On paper, my mother has led an accomplished life. She was a standout in her high school class, active in extracurricular organizations, and voted homecoming queen. My mom attended a small college, Lenoir-Rhyne College, in North Carolina, where, once again, she shined. She was involved in college clubs and her sorority, and she was named Miss Lenoir-Rhyne her junior year. She graduated with a degree in education and became a high school teacher and coach. Her success as a coach earned her an induction into the Stonewall Jackson High School Hall of Fame.

My mom and dad got divorced when I was very young, and because of the divorce, she needed to support both of us. She went back to college and worked towards a master's in education to go into school administration and make more money. She graduated and became the first female assistant principal in Shenandoah County, Virginia. She got paid less than her male counterparts, as it was the 1980s and sexual discrimination was still rampant in small-town Virginia, but she did it and provided well for the two of us. She later became a high school principal (*my* principal) and handed me my high school diploma at graduation. I am proud of her for all that she has accomplished and endured.

So, to hear my mom say, "I never really knew what I was meant to do with my life, so I just tried to make other people happy," made the years of darkness and struggle I had endured with this same problem come flooding back. It also gave me a strange sense of solace and comfort, knowing that I needed to share what I have learned with others.

I have spent many years struggling to answer that elusive question: *what am I meant to do?* I felt like a failure because I could not answer it, especially when I saw others around me who seemed to know from day one what they were meant to do.

WHAT AM I MEANT TO DO?

I struggled with this question for so many years, and it is only recently that I finally understood why I could never find the answer. *It's the wrong question*, at least to start with. To know what you are meant to do, you must first answer this question: *who am I?*

WHO AM I?

If you do not know who you are—I mean, deep down, right at the raw core know the wake-up-in-the-middle-of-the-night-and-it's-only-you *you*—then there is no way you can know what you're meant to do in this world. As this book will show, everything in your world shapes who you are, and most of us are not even aware of it.

If you're like me, you're probably asking yourself, *Why should I take the time to read this book and listen to anything this guy has to say on this topic?*

Great question. I don't have a degree in psychology, I have no formal training related to helping people find their life purpose, I haven't spent years attending silent retreats, and I am not a world-famous speaker or life coach. By all normal measures, I am pretty ordinary.

Except, I have lived it.

Everything I am sharing with you is something I have lived through and learned through personal experience, struggle, and falling flat on my face. Moving forward, you will see that I have trolled my own personal pits of despair, I have explored my past for the clues as to who I am, I have cried and felt overwhelmed, ashamed, and embarrassed of things I didn't do and things I should not have done. I have reached milestones that I thought would be mountaintops, only to realize they didn't make me happy at all. When I didn't want to get back up or didn't know where to go next, some beautiful people supported and guided me. The truth is, discovering who you are is not a journey you can walk completely on your own. This book, what you are holding, is what I learned along the way, and I hope that it will help you discover exactly who *you* are and what you are meant to do.

CHAPTER 2

THE EQUATION

No one sits you down and teaches you what makes you *you* in a clear and concise manner. There is a lot of talk and hand-waving, birds and bees, family values, references to individuality, and talk of authenticity, which can all be great, but also confusing.

For many years, I struggled to wrap my head around all that I was learning. It is a well-known fact that the human mind cannot hold or process lists of more than about three to five things at any given point in time. My mind was completely overwhelmed by the notion of trying to answer one of the most complex and philosophical questions that has ever been asked: *who am I?*

And then, on June 11, 2019, something happened.

On my best days, I have a routine of waking up, doing a twenty-minute meditation, and then opening my notebook for morning gratitudes and a journaling session. On that particular morning, I began to journal about how we define ourselves as humans. We have been taught to create definitions through comparison and contrast, to look *out*, observe those around us, and see how we are the same or different from what we see. This makes sense as the entire scientific classification system is built upon identifying differences.

However, what struck me that day, was that we Beings are all much more similar than we are different, on a biological level. Which made me ask, *what really makes us different from one another?* And then, I started to write an equation—the Being Equation. In looking for what makes each of us different, I had stumbled upon five variables that define what makes each of us uniquely who we are, that answer the question: *who am I?* In that moment, I felt electric, and this equation became all I could think about over the next few days.

After three days of thinking and writing about the Being Equation, I had to discuss it with someone. I asked my wife, Christi, if she had ten minutes to spare so that I could run an idea by her. We were still talking about it three hours later.

This book is the culmination of my thinking and writing about the Being Equation since that day.

What took me a few more months to understand was why this information came out as a mathematical equation. I had never created or journaled about equations in the past, or since, for that matter. So, why an equation in this case? One day, the answer came to me.

Dr. Hans Jenny, a soil scientist, published a book in 1941 titled, *Factors of Soil Formation: A System of Quantitative Pedology*. In this book, Dr. Jenny takes the complexity of thousands of different soil types, spread all over the globe, and reduces them to five variables that can be used to define any given soil in the world. When I was studying ecology, not only did I use Dr. Jenny's equation to understand soil, but I also used it as a conceptual framework for understanding all the different ecosystems on the planet.

I realized in hindsight that my subconscious must have reached a conclusion: if an equation works to define thousands of soils and all the ecosystems on the planet, why shouldn't one work to define what makes us all uniquely who we are? Thus, the Being Equation was created. Although I never met Dr. Jenny in person, I owe him a deep debt of gratitude. Thank you, Dr. Jenny.

If you are not into math, please do not let the Being Equation scare you. Think of it as five categories that shape your life and make you who you are. In a general sense, you can think of these variables as Spirit, Physical Body, Inputs, Life Events, and Egoic Interpretation.

Put in non-mathematical terms, every living being at any moment in time can be thought of as a unique combination of Spirit and a Spiritual Body that is joined to a Physical Body, created through our parents' genetics. This Spiritual/Physical combination grows and develops through the environmental and Physical Inputs it receives. This Spiritual, biological, and environmental mix is then formed, molded, and shaped by every Life Event and the Egoic Interpretation, or Story, we tell ourselves about those Life Events. This represents who you are at any moment in time. By knowing who you are in the present moment, you can start exploring what you're meant to do.

For me, thinking of this as a mathematical equation is practical. Maybe it will be helpful for you, too.

THE BEING EQUATION

$$B_x(t) = f(SPIL_xE_x)$$

B_x = Being

(t) = Time (t)

f = A mathematical term representing "function of" or "dependent on"

S = Spirit—Combination of Source Energy and Spiritual Body

P = Physical Body—Genetics and Epigenetics of Being

I = Inputs—Physical and Environmental Inputs of Being

L_x = Life Events

E_x = Egoic Interpretation of Life Events

WHAT DOES IT ALL MEAN?

Through the structure of the Being Equation, you will know what makes you *you*. First, you will identify your current foundational beliefs in each of the five categories of the Being Equation. Second, you will challenge each belief and decide if each aligns with who you are at your core. In my case, they were not in alignment, which created a life of struggle. This realization changed my life, and I believe with all my Being, it can change yours, too.

Every decision we make, every area in which we work to gain clarity, is built upon a foundation that most of us never explore or question. Our clarity is built upon an underlying foundation of

First Principles, truths, or assumptions that we believe to be true about the world. *Whether you know it or not, you have an underlying subconscious program, a filter of sorts, through which all of your decisions about everything in your life are funneled before you ever consciously make a decision.* The basis for this filtering system is your First Principles.

FIRST PRINCIPLES

The concept of First Principles is fundamental to understand before we move forward. The concept is originally attributed to Aristotle. Many great thinkers and inventors throughout history have used First Principle thinking, including Johannes Gutenberg, Thomas Edison, Richard Feynman, Nikola Tesla, and Elon Musk (to drop a few names).

Aristotle defined First Principles as "the first basics from which a thing is known." In an episode of *The TED Interview*, Elon Musk describes how he uses First Principles to "boil things down to their fundamental truths and reason up from there, as opposed to reasoning by analogy. *Through most of our life, we get through life by reasoning by analogy, which essentially means copying what other people do with slight variations.*"[1]

For me, a magic moment occurred when I finally realized that all of the clarity I thought I had in my life was built upon a set of First Principles that was not aligned with who I truly am at my core. This created confusion and depression: reaching the wrong mountain-tops and, in the vernacular of Napoleon Hill, "the drifting."

And there is the crux of it all—the reason why First Principle inter-

---

1   Elon Musk, "The mind behind Tesla, SpaceX, SolarCity...", TED, accessed February 23, 2021, https://www.ted.com/talks/elon_musk_the_mind_behind_tesla_spacex_solarcity#t-4566.

pretation is so critical to understanding the context of the Being Equation and life in general.

The Being Equation is *who you are on a First Principle level.* The five variables of the Being Equation are the most basic, fundamental building blocks that make you *you.* We will use First Principle thinking to challenge our understanding and assumptions about what we believe to be true about each of these five variables for each of us. That is because *the vast majority of us are living by analogy, meaning we are copying what other people do around us, assuming that is who we are as well.*

This is the fundamental fly in the ointment and the reason why so many people, myself included, have struggled so mightily with what we are meant to do. We live our lives built upon others' beliefs and values without even realizing that these beliefs and values may not be our own. This is natural because the way we traditionally learn, starting in infancy, is to follow by example or be taught information by our parents and peers. Back in the days of the caveman, you didn't just walk out the door to kill a saber-toothed tiger by trial and error. You did not wing it. You watched and learned from others whom you deemed successful at hunting saber-toothed tigers.

My life of clarity was built on the wrong First Principles. As I mentioned, my mother and father divorced when I was too young to consciously remember. They were both educators. At the time, my mother was a teacher, and she later became an assistant principal and then principal of the high school I attended. My father was also a teacher, so education played an important role in my upbringing. From an early age, I learned that I needed to work hard, get good grades, and go to college.

All through elementary, middle, and high school, I was a good student academically. I was nearly always in the top 10 percent of my class and was accepted to the three colleges I applied to. I never really had any idea what I wanted to do as a profession, but in high school, I enjoyed biology, so when I got to college, biology seemed as good a major as any. I rushed to make a decision because I believed that you could only stay undecided for so long.

The problem was that, at my university, the biology program was primarily geared towards pre-medical studies, meaning that it focused on turning out machines ready to take the MCAT. I still had no idea what I wanted to be, but I definitely did *not* want to be a doctor. I switched majors and decided to study geology because the department was small, and one of the geology professors had taken some time to talk to me.

I had never studied geology before, but I liked nature. It seemed closely related to biology, some of my credits transferred to the major, there were some fun people in the program, and I got to spend time outside. And that is how I ended up with a degree in geology.

What did I do with my newly completed geology degree? I went to work as a gardener in North Carolina, making seven dollars an hour, because the job was close to my girlfriend, destined to be my wife, and what the hell was I supposed to do with a geology degree anyway? After a year or so, I needed to make more money, so a friend connected me with a medical consulting firm. The pay was more than double my seven dollars an hour, and we needed money, so I took the job. After a year of installing computer healthcare software and working in inventory management, I got hired by another consulting firm to travel to other hospitals around the country and be the "expert consultant"—doing the same thing I had been doing for fifteen dollars an hour. Except these people charged the hospitals big daily consulting fees for my time, and they paid me a lot more than I had been making. Plus, they flew me around the country every week, which was exciting for about two months. What did this have to do with that geology degree? Nothing.

Add two years and thirty more pounds on my body, and I was finally miserable enough to leave the jetsetter consulting lifestyle and become a teller at a bank in a grocery store. Why? Because I didn't want to travel anymore, and the people at the bank said they would hire me. It was as simple as that. So, as my wife and I sat on the beach in Grenada on our honeymoon, I told her I was quitting my consulting job as soon as we got back. It had generally been our plan, but I think she was surprised by the speed at which I executed it upon our return from the honeymoon.

After eight months at the bank, I knew the teller life was not for me, so I did the only thing I knew to do to advance my life. I went back to school to improve my education. This time, I ended up studying ecology. Why ecology? I had a friend from undergrad who was studying ecology at Colorado State University. I liked nature, had always wanted to live in Colorado, and ecology seemed like a good blend of biology and geology. My amazing and supportive wife resigned from her job at Duke University, loaded up a Penske truck, and moved to Colorado with me.

I spent the next three years studying rangeland ecology and the effects of overgrazing on soil and ecosystem health. Sounds interesting, right? Did I have a deep interest in rangelands or soils, for that matter? No, but a professor had a graduate research stipend available for studying rangeland ecology, so that is what I did.

After earning my master's degree in rangeland ecology, I did wind up doing some interesting scientific work with Colorado State University and USDA Agricultural Research Service, getting the chance to work with some amazing folks. Ultimately, I decided the world of scientific research within the confines of the federal government was not for me, so I did the only thing I knew to do: I went back to graduate school and got an MBA. Not because I liked business, but because it was the most flexible degree possible, and I could complete it on nights and weekends.

Every time I got miserable in a job, I thought more education and a new job would make me happy. I would get the degree, the new job, and guess what? I still wasn't happy. I kept doing the only thing I knew to solve the problem: get more education.

I could keep going, but I believe that I have gone far enough for you to see the flaw. I had clarity built on an incorrect First Principle. Because of the way I was raised and saw the world, I believed formal education was always the answer to improving your life. If you wanted to advance or change, you had to be educated. Thus, I have two advanced degrees that I do not formally use.

I would have been so much better served by gaining clarity on what was controlling my need for more education instead of acting on my *assumed* clarity of being able to improve my life through it.

This story highlights a point that is often missed: most people are good at achieving goals; however, they never truly achieve *their* goals because they do not know what *their* goals are. They have goals they think are theirs, but at the core, they are not their goals at all. They are their parents' goals, society's goals, or their friends' goals, and they cannot see what they truly want.

To know what your goals are, you must first know who you are. You will find happiness and contentment when you start achieving *your* goals instead of the goals of others—the ones you assume are yours.

Need a bit more proof? How many rich people do you know who are miserable? Or can you think of a friend or acquaintance who you used to think was "successful," but you later found out that the person was fundamentally unhappy? They had the spouse, the job, the kids, the car, the house, the country club membership, and all the trappings of success, but they were unfulfilled. I would bet you a new, shiny nickel that the reason they were miserable is that they had never probed deep enough to determine if all those things were what *they* desired at their core. My bet is that guy with the seven-figure salary and the Ferrari, working eighty hours a week, probably has no idea why he is really doing any of it.

As I have said, our wants and desires are often based on what we have been told we should want by others and society, and we do not realize at a conscious level that our desires are not truly our own. They were given to us by others. However, at a subconscious level, our true self knows that "our" perceived desires are not in alignment with who we are.

The following chapters give you an in-depth look at each of the five variables of the Being Equation. Once you understand the Being Equation and how the variables interact, you will have the knowledge to begin creating your life. You will realize that, if you want to change your life, all you have to do is change any variable in the Being Equation. This book shows you how to start doing it and gives you the power to shape the Being you want to become.

CHAPTER 3

SPIRIT

$$B_x(t) = f(SPIL_xE_x)$$

S = Spirit—combination of Source Energy and Spiritual Body

WHO OR WHAT IS SPIRIT?

We might as well jump straight into the deep end, so let's start with the variable that may seem the most controversial to some—Spirit.

Whenever I think of how to address a discussion of Spirit, Source Energy, and Spiritual Body in the Being Equation, I remember a question and answer that is often attributed to Albert Einstein but cannot be definitively linked to him, which seems fitting. The question is: "is the universe a friendly place?" Einstein's supposed response is that your perspective on this question will shape and determine your answer.

The question of Spirit, Source Energy, and Spiritual Body is much the same. If you believe there is a Spiritual component to all of this, then you will see the connections and the synchronicities throughout your life. You will find examples of the spiritual connection we all share. On the other hand, if you believe that all Spirituality and the idea of some super-being creator is made up to explain our existence, then you will have endless evidence supporting your belief.

As a person who has a long history with the scientific method and education on evolution, I can use my logical mind to rationalize both sides. There is no indisputable, overwhelming scientific evidence that can prove the existence of Spirit or any type of unifying force that can be measured. The fossil record and multiple studies over the last few hundred years sure lend a lot of evidence to the idea that we originated from the primordial soup and this whole Spirit thing is just a way to make us feel good and accept that death, which is coming for all of us, is not the end.

The truth is that there is no way, with our current level of technology and understanding, to scientifically prove the existence of Spirit or anything Spiritually-related. However, it is also true that with our current level of technology and understanding, there is no way we can scientifically *disprove* the existence of Spirit or anything Spiritually-related.

The bottom line is the existence of Spirit can neither be proven nor disproven, and that is why I like Einstein's supposed framing in this context. If you believe there is Spirit within all of us, then in your world, it will appear to be so. And if you don't believe in any of that, in your world, it will also appear to be so.

Before we go any further, I would like to take a moment to clarify the way I use the term "Spirit" throughout this book because it does have different meanings to different people. When I use the term Spirit, I am referring to the unique Spirit that is *within* each of us. Some people use the word Spirit as a replacement for "God" or "Creator" that is *external* to you. Your individual Spirit is the combination of Source Energy and your Spiritual Body. I will cover this in more detail, but I think it is essential to keep this distinction in mind as we move forward. And it is especially important here for you not to confuse Spirituality with religion or the creator concept.

You do not have to believe in a creator or religion to have a Spirit and a Spiritual Body. We have all had the experience of feeling refreshed and recharged after some time in nature or a walk outdoors, or for you, maybe it comes from sitting and staring at the ocean. There is a part inside us that needs something other than food and water to be replenished. That is your Spiritual Body. If you're still skeptical, that's okay. Just hang with me and see how you feel by the end of the chapter.

The easiest way to think about the relationship between Spirit, Source Energy, and Spiritual Body is to equate it to a Physical Body. Source Energy is like the initial DNA that is in that first cell of our Physical Body. This initial Source Energy contains the entire "DNA" that forms the basis for your Spiritual Body. It just so happens that instead of each of us having unique DNA, like for our Physical Bodies, we all have the same Spiritual DNA that forms the basis for our Spiritual Body. Just as our Physical Bodies are shaped by all of the Inputs from this point forward, so are our Spiritual Bodies. Our Spiritual Bodies grow and form, just as our Physical Bodies grow and form.

As food and water is the energy for our Physical Body, Spiritual Energy is the fuel for our Spiritual Body. Contemplating the enormity and ubiquitous nature of Spiritual Energy is like trying to discuss the importance and nature of water. Like water, I believe that Spiritual Energy is in every living being, and Spiritual Energy fuels the Spiritual Body. We can't see the water inside us, but we know it makes up most of our bodies. We start to feel "off" when we don't replenish and recharge our water, and without water, we die. I think of Spiritual Energy in much the same way.

SPIRITUAL ENERGY

Every living being has Spiritual Energy inside of them, and like taking a drink of water, we can take actions to recharge our Spiritual Energy when it starts to feel low. Just as going for a run on a hot day drains lots of water from your body, there are activities and situations that draw heavily on your Spiritual Energy. Like drinking a tall, icy refreshing glass of water after a run, there are places and practices that can recharge your Spiritual Energy, and we will discuss these further in later chapters.

It's most important now that you are aware that you have a Spirit and a Spiritual Body. Your Spirit and Spiritual Body do not have to have anything to do with religion unless you choose that path. However, you do have to acknowledge and nourish your Spirit as it forms an integral part of who you are. As you'll see in later chapters, there are many ways to connect with and nourish your Spirit, and in Chapter 15, I've included exercises related explicitly to exploring your Spirit.

Take some time to think about this chapter thus far and see your underlying First Principles as they relate to Spirit.

To give you some insight and an example to explore your First Principles, here is a bit about my own journey with the interplay between Spirituality and religion and how it formed my First Principles and my relationship to Spirit.

I grew up in a small town in Virginia, a tiny town where everyone knew everyone and generations of families stayed in the same area. We were Lutherans. My grandmother played the pipe organ at church on Sundays, and my mother sang in the church choir.

I got drunk for the first time at the age of four on leftover communion wine (an innocent accident, but that is another story). The Lutheran Church left a permanent mark on me when, at the age of five, I was stabbed in my left cheek with a pencil by my Sunday school classmate. I still have the lead in my cheek to prove it. Our community was religiously diverse (ha ha!). Besides Lutherans, there were also Methodists and Presbyterians. I had heard there were other religions out there, but I had never seen a real-life practitioner of another religion in person until well into high school. The point of all this being: my understanding at the time was that religion was not a choice you made; you were born into it. I was born into a Lutheran family, so I was Lutheran. *Can you see how my First Principle around religion (and Spirituality), that I was a Lutheran, developed and I accepted it without even knowing I had made a decision?*

SPIRITUALITY

I know talking about religion and Spirituality can be a difficult topic. I want to be careful not to lose you because I believe the rest of this book can change your life. In essence, *I don't want you to throw the baby out with the bathwater on this one. If you have had enough of Spirit at this point, then move on to the next chapter and perhaps come back to this later.*

What follows is a more in-depth look at my personal understanding of the interaction between Spirit, Spirituality, and religion, and some of my personal experiences. If you are curious, then read on. I talk generally about religions, so please remember this is only my view. I am not trying to change yours.

For me, the idea of Spirit goes back to the word "creator." I believe that, out there, somewhere, there is one big pot of Source Energy from which all things have been, are, and will be created. We each have a little dab of this pure Source Energy within us, which is why each and every living being is a powerful creator. We are all made of the same Source Energy, and, as such, we can create our worlds. Some Beings are more aware of this power than others.

Here is a breakdown:

1. Every living Being is imbued with Source Energy.
2. Source Energy retains the Source's properties (Spiritual DNA), meaning that we are powerful creators with the ability to create and shape our worlds.
3. We need to nurture and develop our Spiritual Body just as we nurture and take care of our Physical Body.

SOURCE AND SOURCE ENERGY

I want to take a moment and clarify the relationship between Source and Source Energy. Source can be thought of as the origin of all Source Energy, and it is not something that can be described with language or imagined by the mind. Source can only be felt and intuited. Every living Being that is, was, or will be contains Source Energy, all drawn from the same Source.

It is critical to understand that every living being is a piece of Source, and just like each cell in our body contains the entire genetic code for a human, each of us contains a complete copy of Source. We just activate and initiate it differently as individuals, as we see through the application of the Being Equation.

Let me be direct. What I am about to say may not feel comfortable to you at first. It may be disconcerting, but stick with me.

We all have the same Source Energy.

That is, we all have the exact same Spiritual DNA. Since we all come from the same Source, we all contain the exact same Source Energy. We cannot change our Source Energy; it is fixed, a constant. I can just hear the questions and objections leaping forth from your mind as this sentence lands. Because we all want to be unique, it is jarring to acknowledge that your Source Energy is not unique.

I had a very hard time accepting this myself until I looked at it from the following perspective: if your Source Energy were unique, it would mean that your life was at least partially pre-determined. Your capacity as a Spiritual Being would be pre-determined by the value of your Source Energy. I do not believe that our lives are pre-determined in any manner or that we each have a pre-determined fate or destiny. Source Energy has to be the same for every Being in order for our fate not to be pre-determined.

Do not confuse Source Energy with Spiritual Body, Spirituality, or religion. Source Energy for every single Being that ever was, is, or will be, has the exact same value regardless of that Being's level of Spirituality or religion. Large, organized religions as we know them only started a few thousand years ago. What about all of the Beings that existed before religions existed? Were they denied their Source Energy because no religion existed to inform them about the Spirit or Spirituality? As some religions imply, were these Beings subject to eternal damnation because they had not accepted a savior they knew nothing about? This same question exists today about religion, and I will address it shortly.

This is a good time to introduce you to a practice that I follow when I am seeking clarity or answers to questions that I don't know how to answer. I open my journal and start writing a dialogue as if I were sitting across the table from another person, except my dialogue is with Source. To be honest, I didn't know how to address Spirit in the context of religions, so I sat down, opened my journal, put my pen in my hand, and asked Source how to address it in the context of religion. Below is the dialogue I had with Source on this topic.

A CONVERSATION WITH SOURCE

Me: Source, how do you want to be addressed in the context of religion?

Source: Religion has been a way for human beings to try to understand Spirit. Human beings can feel Spirit, but they just can't wrap their heads around the practical side of it because Spirit can't be defined in the terms usually used to describe other aspects of the world. There is nothing else on the planet, no other type of matter, quark, or electron that is like Spirit. It doesn't adhere to any of the laws human beings have defined.

The laws man has created come from the mind, logic, classification, and reduction. You can't use the mind as a tool to understand Spirit. It would be like trying to pick a paint color for your house with your ears. Human beings know how the ear works on a mechanical level. They know how sound waves enter the ear, cause vibrations in the cochlea, and move the tympanum, which transmits electrical impulses through neurons to the auditory cortex of the temporal lobe of the brain, where it is interpreted as sound. Human beings understand the physics of how sound travels through air and how the density of air, or any material, affects how sound travels. Human beings have mathematical formulas describing and predicting, to the minutest measurement and detail, the exact nature and behavior of sound. In fact, human beings could use sound and the reflection of sound, known as radar, to give the exact shape, size, and location of a house. Still, even with all that knowledge and understanding, there is no way humans could use their ears to determine the house's current color or what color it should be painted. Your ears are the wrong system for choosing a paint color, and no amount of information will change that.

This is also true for Spirit. You, as a human, can feel Spirit. Some of you are much more sensitive to it than others. Still, as soon as you try to put Spirit into a conceptual framework that is universally accepted, like the physical laws of sound, the concept breaks down because Spirit can't be measured by any instruments that exist in human conception.

Me: Okay, but why is Spirit viewed so differently by so many religions?

Source: The truth is that Spirit is universally the same across all of them. Remember that when different religions emerged in various parts of the world, people were not connected; people and cultures were isolated.

Everyone can *feel* Spirit. There are as many different ways that Spirit can be expressed as there are people in the world because there is no universal or defining measure of Spirit. Look, human beings are here for experience. They learn and grow through experience, and they want to share and express themselves through experience. Human beings encounter Spirit every day because Spirit is within them. It is part of all living Beings. Some human beings are more open and receptive to what Spirit has to share and have tried to share what they have learned with others. What each person receives and shares is always within their culture because this is what they know—the only framework, the only language, and the only landscape they know.

Humans have learned a tremendous amount about the physical world over the past few thousand years, but for all the gains in knowledge of the physical world, there has been a decrease in knowledge and connection to the Spiritual world. All living Beings contain Spirit. Humans have used their increasing knowledge of the physical world to seal themselves off and isolate themselves from the natural world, from their connection to plants and animals, and the cycle of all living Beings. There is less connection with the natural cycle of seasons. Humans have heating and cooling to keep the temperature at sixty-six degrees Fahrenheit year-round inside their sealed-up homes. They have electricity and lights to maintain a consistent sixteen hours of daylight. They don't rise with the sun and sleep when it is dark anymore. I (Source) will say this once and for all, but it will not matter: it will never be possible to measure Spirit with any instrument created by human beings. There is no one place that Spirit resides because it is everyplace.

Me: So, back to religion. Why do religions arise then? Why is there not one universal definition or understanding of Spirit?

Source: Religions are the product of a human being's Spiritual understanding at a given point in time. This understanding is then shared through language and communication and, most importantly, the culture of the time. Then other humans start to share, expand, and add their own pieces of knowledge and understanding to it. For example, in the past, squirrels only lived in forests and had no understanding of skyscrapers, towns, and cities, but the squirrels of today can live in cities and know about cars because their Story has changed as their environment has changed. There are examples of this throughout the natural world. Humans are no different.

Reader's note: In this dialogue, Source uses the word "Story." To preserve the original dialogue, this Reader's note is inserted to define Story in this context. Story is simply the view or understanding that a Being has about the world and how they exist in it.

What human beings do that other Beings do not is try to use Story to gain power and control over other Beings. A lion will kill and eat what it needs in the moment, but no more. It does not kill for show. A bird will take just enough grass and twigs to build a nest big enough for itself and its offspring, not a nest ten times bigger than it needs to show the other birds how great it is. No other Beings besides human beings use Story to control others. Humans have a bad habit of trying to do this, and when religion is used to justify control, its original intent is corrupted.

Me: So, where does that leave humans on what they should think about religion?

Source: If a religion originated from a place of pure Spiritual intention, trying to understand and connect with Spirit, then there is truth within it. It is up to each Spiritual Being to decide what truth connects with them. *The trouble is that most human beings have forgotten how to think and feel for themselves. They want to be told what to feel and think.* Human beings also think you must accept the whole story or none of it, or every aspect of the religion or none of it. This is not the case, but do not misconstrue this to mean that you can accept what is convenient and discard what is inconvenient. Far from it. You can accept what you feel and know with your Spirit to be true and discard what you feel and know with your Spirit not to be true. Trust your Spirit.

This is the conclusion of this dialog with Source.

This written conversation helped me better understand my relationship with Spirit and human beings' current and historical relationship with Spirit.

I am not here to support or condemn any religion. In my view, the actions you take and how you show up in the world is ultimately your religion, meaning your actions speak far louder than your words when it comes to what you believe. Unfortunately, many examples abound with supposedly devout people acting in ways in complete discordance with their religion.

Religions are guides, but you are a Spiritual Being on your own, unique path. Trust your Spirit.

QUESTIONS TO CONSIDER

- Can you think of something that recharges your Spiritual Energy?
- Have you been automatically connecting Spirit and religion?
- Have you turned away from your Spirit because of a negative religious experience?
- Have you connected with your Spirit because of a positive religious experience?
- Do you believe you can have a Spiritual practice without being religious?

CHAPTER 4

PHYSICAL BODY

$$B_x(t) = f(SPIL_xE_x)$$

P = Physical Body—Genetics and Epigenetics of Being

Have you ever deeply thought about where your Physical Body comes from and what controls its development? Your Physical Body forms the basis of how you interact with every Being and every thing in the physical world, and how other Beings see and interact with you. Your experience as a Being comes through your five physical senses, so understanding the Physical Body and the role it plays in the Being Equation and forming who you are is critical.

Just as Source Energy represents the Source DNA that forms our

Spiritual Body, the genetics and epigenetics of each Being provide the literal DNA that supplies the template for the Physical Body.

We all know that the genes we receive from our parents set the starting point for our Physical Body, but they also can control so much more. Understanding genetics—the branch of biology concerned with the study of genes, genetic variation and heredity in organisms, and epigenetics; the study of changes in organisms caused by modification of gene expression rather than alteration of the genetic code itself—is critical to understanding the forces that create who we are.

This chapter will delve into the science of genetics and epigenetics, and before we go too deep down that rabbit hole, I want to make one point clear: some of our physical traits are fixed by our DNA, like eye color and hair color. However, for other physical traits, DNA only sets a spectrum of possibility, and the physical trait is the result of much more that is in our control, like physical stature or even height. You are in control of much more than you may realize.

Although the classic scientific approach has been one that trends towards reductionism, or studying smaller and smaller segments in isolation, the role of genetics, gene expression, and genetic variation needs to be viewed in the context of the environment and the environmental conditions in which the organism lives. There has long been discussion of the role of nurture versus nature in determining an organism's physical and behavioral expression of genes. We now realize that genes can be turned on or off based on both behavioral and environmental conditions.

A BRIEF LESSON ON GENETICS

The phenomenon of nurture is exhibited in a classic study in which two genetically identical plants (this experiment holds "nature" constant by using genetically identical individuals) are planted in two different environments, one arid and nutrient-limited (low nurture) and one humid and nutrient-rich (high nurture). Although the plants are genetically identical, the one in the arid environment (low nurture) only grows to half the size of the humid environment (high nurture). This experiment shows the role nurture plays in determining the ability of an organism to reach its full genetic potential.

A direct example of nature is more difficult to provide, and this difficulty points to a simple truth. It is not possible to separate the role of nature versus nurture in determining the identity traits of an individual. The genetics, the nature, of an individual directly influences the response to the nurture, external rearing or forming, and vice versa. Who we are as individuals is a combination of both nature and nurture.

To give some context to genetics, let's briefly talk about the history of genetics. Some of the earliest writing in the field of genetics and heredity comes from the famous Hindu text, the *Charaka Samhita*, dating from around the second century BCE. The *Charaka Samhita* identified four factors in determining the characteristics of human offspring.

Those factors include:

1. Those from the mother's reproductive material.
2. Those from the father's sperm.
3. Those from the diet of the pregnant mother.
4. Those accompanying the soul that enters the fetus.[2]

Later, works by Hippocrates and Aristotle, amongst others, during

---

2   Bhagwan Bhagwan and R. K. Sharma, *Charaka Samhita* (Chowkhamba Sanskrit Series, 2009), pp. sharirasthanam II, 26–27.

the classical period from the eighth to sixth centuries BCE, are credited with forming the basis of scientific knowledge in the fields of genetics and heredity in the West.[3] In the mid-1800s, the famous Charles Darwin put forward his theory on genetics, coined pangenesis. During this same general time, Gregor Mendel, an Augustinian friar who lived from 1822 to 1884, put forth his theories of genetics in a scientific paper published in 1866.[4] However, his theory only gained prominence more than three decades after his death, when it was "rediscovered" by three researchers in the early 1900s. This rediscovery of Mendel's work led to Mendel being considered the "father" of the field of genetics and to the proverbial floodgates opening in the field with the discovery of chromosomes in 1910, DNA in the 1940s, and the famous double helix structure of DNA in 1952, leading to the field of molecular biology. The first gene was sequenced in 1972, and now, since 2019, you can swab your cheek and have your genome sequenced for about one hundred dollars.

THE TRUTH ABOUT DNA

So, why the history lesson on genetics? Each generation of human beings and scientific researchers thought they were on the cutting edge of knowledge and understanding, not just in genetics, but in all topics. We, as humans, have a history of thinking we are always on the cutting edge of understanding, and the suppositions we make from our understanding must be the truth. Our current level of understanding around genetics and the language we use exhibits this paradigm. Our genetic blueprint consists of 3.42 billion nucleotides arranged in twenty-three pairs of linear chromosomes. The variability in quantity and arrangement of nucleotides amongst species is vast, with no apparent connection being obvious between

---

3   A. H. Sturtevant, *A History of Genetics* (New York: Harper and Row, 1965).

4   Gregor Mendel, *Versuche über Pflanzenhybriden.* Verhandlungen des naturforschenden Vereines in Brünn, Bd. IV für das Jahr 1865, Abhandlungen, 3–47.

the size of individuals within a species and the quantity of nucleotides comprising their DNA or a correlation between the number of genes and complexity, and only a small percentage of an organism's DNA codes for proteins used to build bodies and catalyze reactions in cells. *Estimates of the percentage vary amongst scientists, but the current estimate is that only 2–8 percent of our DNA has a function under this definition.* No one really knows the purpose for the remaining 92–98 percent of our DNA.

Think about that for a second.

We are on the cutting edge of technology and can now sequence the entire genome of all living organisms on the planet but only know the purpose of 2–8 percent of our DNA. And since we don't know what this other 92–98 percent of our DNA does, scientists and researchers have labeled it "junk DNA." The commonly accepted term for this huge portion of our DNA speaks volumes as to how things that are not understood within science get labeled as insignificant or unimportant. The 92–98 percent we don't understand is junk in the eyes of science. It may have some purpose, but until the purpose is known, it's junk. That would be like reading this paragraph, which is 188 words long, and only being able to read four words, and deciding the other 184 must be junk because you don't know what they mean, and you do not know their purpose. There is a major flaw in this logic, and if you, as the reader, do not see it, I don't believe I will be able to make it any clearer for you in another 188 words.

However, what may make it a bit clearer is a quote from one of the scientists involved in the study of said "junk DNA." In a 2012 article from *Scientific American* entitled "Hidden Treasures in Junk DNA,"[5] computational biologist Ewan Birney sums up the relative

---

5   Stephen S. Hall, "Journey to the Genetic Interior" *Scientific American* 307, no. 4 (October 2012): 80-85.

level of understanding about junk DNA in the field of genetics. He says, "I get this strong feeling that previously I was ignorant of my own ignorance, and now I understand my ignorance. It's slightly depressing as you realize how ignorant you are. But this is progress. The first step in understanding these things is having a list of things that one has to understand, and that's what we've got here." Read this again and think about it.

With all of this said, how do I treat the "genetic" component of the Being Equation? The physical genetic component of each individual plays a role in determining the Beings that we are. We can look at parents and their offspring and visually see the physical similarities. Through the science of genetics, we definitely know that the genetic makeup of the parent organism gets transferred from each parent to the offspring and that these expressed traits play an important role in the physical expression of the Being.

Where things get dodgy and go far beyond my ability, and the ability of what we as humans understand, is exactly how much our genetics control the expression of who we are. What I mean by this is that we can use genetics to predict certain physical characteristics like eye color, hair color, skin color, etc., but ultimately, there are far more intangible variables, some that we know and some we do not know, that also play a role in determining these things. We base our science on odds, and that is why computational biology is involved in genetics, because scientists crunch big numbers on populations and make predictions based on the outcomes they observe. They predict outcomes for an individual based on results they have observed in a huge population. They cannot predict a specific outcome for an individual. Put another way, a geneticist could have the entire genome of parent one and the entire genome of parent two and could know every bit of genetic information about each parent, yet given this information, they still cannot definitively, with 100 percent certainty, tell you exactly what offspring one will look like. Further, if parent one and parent two produce multiple offspring from the same fertilization event, and those offspring do not originate through identical twinning, then these offspring could have completely different genetics.

Think about this for a minute.

It would make sense that, if parent one is sharing half of their genetic makeup and parent two is sharing half of their genetic makeup, then the genetic makeup they share at any given moment in time should be identical. All of the environmental and life history Inputs that affected that individual all the way up to the exact moment the fertilization event occurred have been 99.999 percent or more identical during the development of the gametes that are present at that particular time. Strictly speaking, from a human standpoint, why is there so much genetic variation in what traits are dominant even from one sperm or one egg to the next within an individual? An average human male can produce between 40 million and 1.2 billion sperm cells in each potential fertilization event. Of this quantity, only one is needed to fertilize a female egg. Each of those 40 million to 1.2 billion, when combined with a female egg, can produce an entirely unique individual, and science cannot definitively say what that individual will look like. Science can only predict with some confidence intervals what they may look like. Science can only give odds.

Why would we evolve with so much variation in our genetic makeup? Why wouldn't each male or female produce an identical set of gametes for any potential reproductive event? Wouldn't it be much simpler that way? What purpose could all of this variation possibly serve? Given our current level of understanding, evolution is the best explanation, and it has been since Darwin put it forth in the mid-1800s.

Regardless of whether Darwin's theory is accurate in explaining how Beings change through time through variation and adaptation to the environment, it does nothing to say why all this variation in genetics is even around in the first place. We are still dealing with and understanding just 2–8 percent. Remember that other 92–98 percent that was junk? Even if the theory of evolution is 100 percent right, it is only explanatory, meaning that it just explains why populations evolve characteristics in the way they do. It does nothing to explain why we have so much variation and so much DNA in the first place or what the other 98 percent of all this DNA does. The theory of evolution is only a plausible explanation for what we understand at this particular point in time. It does nothing to explain why we have so much "extra" DNA in the first place.

As we go through our lives as Beings, we have experiences, and we generate an interpretation of the world through these experiences. The historic way of thinking about reproduction is that reproduction occurs, and the physical traits of the parent Beings, in the case of male and female, come together in some combination to produce an offspring that is a genetic combination of the male and female. The offspring receives all of the physical information from the parents, and then it is up to the offspring to use those physical characteristics to the best of its ability to learn about and thrive in the environment. Other than a physical adaptation, we did not think specific behaviors or knowledge were passed from one generation to the next in any other form than "instinct" or a learned behavior, meaning the parent rabbit teaches the offspring rabbits that they should run when a shadow moves overhead.

But what if some of the knowledge the parents had gained throughout their collective lifetimes of experience could be passed along to the offspring without any physical changes in the DNA, but only in changes to which sequences of DNA were turned on or turned off. Think about this for a moment. We have always thought of DNA as physical trait information, with the idea that the traits that make an offspring best suited to an environment will be passed along. But physical traits are only a small portion of the information that an offspring can use to be successful. What about all of the life experiences and practices the parent Being learns through a lifetime of living? What if that information could be passed along as well without having to be taught as a learned behavior? What if innate knowledge of what happened to the parent Being during their lifetime could be shared with the offspring Being? How valuable would the lessons learned during the parent Being's life be to the offspring Being's success?

EPIGENETICS

These questions bring us to epigenetics, the study of changes in organisms caused by modification of gene expression rather than alteration of the genetic code itself.

Every cell in a body contains the entire DNA sequence for that Being. A skin cell, a liver cell, a brain cell, etc. from the same Being all have the same DNA sequence. What differentiates a skin cell from a liver cell from a brain cell is which genes or portions of genes within the DNA sequence get expressed. Another way to think of expression is like an on/off switch. If one portion of the gene is turned on, the trait will be expressed. If that portion of the gene is turned off, that portion of the gene will not be expressed. What is critical to note is that the DNA is not being altered in any way; it is only the expression of the DNA that is changed.

DNA is composed of four fundamental chemical bases: adenine, cytosine, guanine, and thymine. The sequence of these bases forms the instructions for all life functions. Genes can be thought of as specific sequences of these four bases. The specific sequences are instructions for how to make different proteins. Proteins are the triggers for various biological processes. These specific biological processes are what lead to cell specialization and differentiation and what allows Beings to become Beings and do all the specialized things that make them what they are.

For differentiation and specialization to occur, certain genes have to be turned on or off. Keep in mind, the entire DNA sequence is preserved in this process, and the tags that turn genes on and off can theoretically be added or removed at any time. They are little chemical switches that can be turned on and off in response to changing conditions without creating permanent changes in the DNA structure.

Here is what is important to understand about epigenetics and how it is different from the typical understanding of evolution. In traditional genetic evolution, a Being has a genetic change in its DNA that makes it more fit for a particular environment. Let's say a fish has a change in its DNA that makes it brown instead of blue because being brown allows it to hide better from the bigger fish that would like to eat it. Because it can hide better, it lives longer and reproduces more, and it passes along its brown color through its DNA to more offspring, thereby giving its brown offspring a better chance at life and reproduction over its blue counterparts. This is a physical change in DNA that is passed to the offspring.

In epigenetics, the physical structure of the DNA is not changed, but the genes that are turned on and off *are* changed. For many years, it was thought that only physical changes in DNA were passed to offspring, and epigenetic changes (on/off switch) were not passed. However, recent studies show signs that these epigenetic on/off switches potentially pass to offspring as well.

So, what does this all mean?

It makes sense that if there is a way to pass on the physical traits and information to offspring that best suit it to an environment and give it the greatest likelihood of success, then it would also be advantageous to pass along the experiential/cultural information that would help them be most prepared for the world they enter. Kind of a non-verbal communication between parent and offspring saying, *Hey, this all happened to me during my life, so you may want to be prepared for it.* Imagine if you could sit down with your children or grandchildren and tell them all the things that happened to you, what traits or skills they should have for those situations, what they should look out for, and what you enjoyed, both pleasure and pain. That's a super simplification of epigenetics. This could be exactly what is happening, but we just don't have the scientific knowledge to prove it.

In order to bring the topic of epigenetics a little more clearly into focus, let's look at an example. In a study performed on mice, researchers taught male mice to fear the smell of acetophenone, a smell that has been compared to cherries or almonds.[6] The researchers wafted the smell through a small chamber and then gave small electrical shocks to the male mice. The mice eventually learned to associate the smell with pain and shook when in the presence of acetophenone, even when no shock was applied. This same reaction was passed down to the offspring of the male mice. Despite the offspring never having encountered the smell of acetophenone before in their lives, the offspring displayed signs of increased sensitivity and shook when presented with the smell, while offspring of male mice that had gone through no smell conditioning displayed no unusual behavior. The "grandchildren," or third generation

---

6   B. Dias and K. Ressler, "Parental olfactory experience influences behavior and neural structure in subsequent generations," *Nat Neurosci* 17, (2014): 89–96.

descended from these male mice also exhibited this reaction to the smell of acetophenone as well. Researchers are unclear as to how this sensitivity could be passed down through the male sperm, but this is a very basic example of epigenetics.

Due to the complexity that would be required, no official experimental studies regarding epigenetics have taken place in humans, but as our scientific understanding of epigenetics increases, there will likely be a greater understanding of what information is passed from parents to offspring through epigenetics. *At this point, it is important to understand that the environment, the physical and mental stresses that were experienced by your parents, grandparents, and potentially even further back in your genetic lineage, all play a role in shaping the person that you are today through epigenetics.* This does not mean that a parent makes a conscious choice to share this information with their offspring. Quite the contrary. This information is included in the DNA, whether they want it to be or not.

It is a new concept for many that what your parents and grandparents experienced, whether you heard stories or even knew or know your parents, grandparents, or great-grandparents, plays a direct role in shaping the person you are today.

What provides even more food for thought, and is something which you can more directly influence, is that what you are experiencing in your life could be passed to your offspring through epigenetics. Many people intuitively know that the physical health of the parents, especially the mother, at the time leading up to conception and through childbirth and nursing plays a fundamental role in the health of the child.

What may not be obvious, and what epigenetics points towards, is that the mental and emotional well-being of the parents, especially the mother, due to the physical connection, is also critical in determining the health of the child. While most evidence pointing to this connection is anecdotal at this point, as studies involving human subjects fall far outside ethical guidelines, a little good old-fashioned common sense can go a long way here.

Do you think a child would be affected differently by spending nine months in the womb of a mother in a kind, loving, well-supported environment with plenty of resources and minimal outside stress or a stressful, negative environment with conflict and limited resources that cause continuous worry and concern?

I am not a parent, but if I were planning to be, I would certainly focus as much attention on creating a positive and supportive mental and emotional environment as I did on prenatal physical health. If you already have children, reflect on the environment during their conception and prenatal development. It is not something to look back on and feel any sense of judgment. It is simply helpful to understand that just as your epigenetics shape you, your child's epigenetics shapes them, and it may be a useful tool to think about in understanding who they are at this moment in time.

Now that you have a basic scientific understanding of how genetics and epigenetics shape the Being you are today, please also recognize that there is a tremendous amount of information we do not understand when it comes to genetics and epigenetics. This field is constantly expanding, and we appear to be on the cusp of rapid advancements in this field. In Chapter 15, we will discuss how you can specifically affect this variable in the Being Equation.

What I would like you to take away from this discussion are three main points:

1. Genetics and epigenetics are responsible for much more than just our physical characteristics.
2. Epigenetics show us that we can turn certain portions of our DNA on or off without changing our DNA, and we can receive more than physical trait information from our ancestors.
3. The fields of genetics and epigenetics are rapidly evolving and what we know now is likely to change in the future, so always stay curious.

QUESTIONS TO CONSIDER

- What is my relationship to my Physical Body in this present moment?
- Do I like my Physical Body?
- Do I take care of my Physical Body?
- Do I accept that I am in control of my body and appearance, or do I believe I am a victim of my genes?
- Am I realizing my "highest and best" genetic potential, however I define highest and best? (While there is no judgment in this question as to what "highest and best" means, you need to be honest with yourself about what it means to you.)
- Do I view my Physical Body as an asset or a liability? Why?

CHAPTER 5

INPUTS

ENVIRONMENTAL AND PHYSICAL

$$B_x(t) = f(SPIL_xE_x)$$

I = Inputs—Environmental and Physical Inputs of Being

Do you feel differently walking along a deserted beach compared to walking along Fifth Avenue in New York City?

When I think of the effect the environment can have on a Being, the image of a krummholz tree comes to mind. The tree has a gnarled and twisted trunk, completely devoid of limbs on the windward side, while the leeward side is full of limbs, shaped like a medieval parade banner, frozen mid-flap in a strong wind. The harsh environmental conditions and strong winds, almost always originating from the same direction, have combined to literally shape the form of this tree to its environment. This exact tree, had it grown in a different, sheltered environment, with minimal wind and plenty of access to resources, would be the traditional, tall, straight, conical-shaped tree everyone draws as a child. However, in this case, the physical environment has been the only factor responsible for the physical change in shape.

Much like each plant species has optimal growing conditions to produce the maximum health, each Being has an optimal physical environment. Like plants, Beings can and do exist in physical environments that are suboptimal. Unlike plants, humans have the ability to pick up and move when an environment does not suit, but many never consciously think of this as a choice. They believe outside circumstances and the difficulties of moving keep them in a specific place. In most cases, the larger geographic environment— the country, state, or city—one lives in is a choice. Although there are definitely situations, for political or economic reasons, where one does not get to choose where one lives. The impact on a Being in this situation can be just as dramatic as seen in krummholz trees, twisting and shaping a Being into a different form than they would normally take. Like a krummholz tree, these Beings often don't even realize they are being so dramatically shaped by their environment. They are not consciously reacting to the environment. Over time, their environment is shaping them.

The environment, both physical and emotional, that we live in, can have the same dramatic impact on us as Beings. Although the effects are not always as visible as on a krummholz tree, they can be as profound. In this chapter, the discussion will focus only on the physical environment, as the emotional environment will be covered in a later chapter.

ENVIRONMENTAL INPUTS

The Being Equation is designed as a framework for understanding what makes each Being who they are. In the broad, general sense, the physical environment represents the physical world a Being lives and interacts in on a broad basis: the country and city they reside in, the house, the car, the landscape. Does the Being live in a city, the countryside, or the wilderness? Each of these environments has different energies, different vibrations, and affect the Being differently. Every space, place, person, and thing has a frequency, and everything around us creates frequencies. All of these frequencies or "energies" of everything impact and change our individual frequencies. This talk of "frequencies" and "energies" may seem a little woo-woo but hear me out on this.

What does being a New Yorker mean? It means being at the frequency, or at least heavily influenced by, the frequency of New York City. What does being a person anywhere mean? Are we adapting to our environment, or are we coming in tune with the frequency of the place that we live? Do places change, or do things happen that change the frequency of a place? I am in Portland at the moment, and there is a look to the people here, and I think if this place clicks with you, if you like the vibe, then you start to develop a look that matches the vibe. This is why the place and space where you live is so critical.

We can use the states of water to illustrate how it is vibration that drives form. Water, in its purest form, is composed of a single molecule, H_2O. Even though the chemical composition of water does not change, it can have three different states depending on its energetic vibration. In the lowest energetic vibration, it is a solid in the form of ice; in the middle energetic state, it is a liquid in the form of water; and in the highest energetic vibration, it is a gas in the form of water vapor or steam. Are we so different as human beings in relation to our vibration? How can we have different states based on our energetic vibration? Just like the water molecule, at any given point in time, the physical makeup of our body does not change, only our energetic vibration.

To understand this concept, close your eyes and imagine yourself walking down a deserted beach at sunrise. Feel the ocean breeze on your face, smell the salt, feel the sand between your toes.

Now, imagine you are walking down Fifth Avenue in New York City during rush hour. Hear the sound of car horns honking, smell the combination of hot dog stands and vehicle exhaust, feel the press of humans standing next to you as you wait for the light to change at the crosswalk. Do you get a different feeling from simply imagining these two different environments? Now, imagine that you lived in these environments. Do you think the different energies created from the environments, day after day, week after week, year after year, would have an effect on who you are as a Being? Did the physical particles that make up your body change? The point is that everything in your environment, on whatever spatial scale being referenced, produces an energetic vibration that has an effect on you. New York City has a different energetic vibration than a deserted beach, an office has a different vibration than a home, a kitchen has a different energetic vibration than a bedroom, and an organized closet has a different energetic vibration than a disorganized closet. The longer you are exposed to an environment, the greater the impact the vibration of the environment has on you.

Once you start thinking about this, the examples and the impact of these vibrations are everywhere. I have three nieces who live in Brooklyn, New York. They can easily understand and navigate the city. Neither of their parents grew up in New York, and neither of them have accents, but I love talking with my nieces because they were born in Brooklyn, and now they have Brooklyn accents. If their parents had been living in Denver and my nieces had been born in Denver, would they have Brooklyn accents? No, living in that environment has affected the Beings that they are. There was no conscious decision on their part to develop a Brooklyn accent. It was simply a result of their living in the environment of Brooklyn, talking to other people who live in Brooklyn, and growing up in that environment. Imagine how else growing up in Brooklyn compared to growing up in Denver is shaping the Beings they are becoming. Is this a conscious choice on the part of my nieces, or are they being shaped and formed, in part, by their environment, just like a krummholz tree is shaped by its environment?

Comparing the effect a country or city may have on a Being, as the example of my nieces, is fairly dramatic, but changes on a smaller spatial scale can be as or more relevant. For example, my wife and I lived in town for about ten years, and then two years ago, we moved four miles away to a property with more land in a more rural setting. We both enjoyed our home in town. It was on a tree-lined street and close to a park. We went for a walk almost every evening. We spent much of our time outside. Our home was a Craftsman-style bungalow, built in the 1920s. It was a single story with a full basement. The home had a large living room, a kitchen, four bedrooms, two bathrooms, and a recreation room. The front of the home looked out onto the tree-lined street. On each side of the house, there were twenty feet of space and then the houses of each of our neighbors. Out the back door was a fenced yard with a detached two-car garage. There was also a dirt alley behind our house. Our entire lot was 9,500 square feet, which was considered a large lot in town. When we bought the house, the open feel of the home and the lot attracted us. Overall, we had been quite happy there.

In comparison, we now live in our barn. Most of our living space is on the second story, above the horse stalls. We have one bedroom and one bathroom and have about one-third of the finished square footage living space that we did in town. Since we live on the second floor, all of our windows have an elevated view of the surrounding landscape. When I look to the south, I see five acres of horse pasture and a large expanse of sky. To the west, there are fifty acres of open land, a tree-lined irrigation canal, and in the distance, the foothills and mountains. To the north, a few neighboring houses a few hundred feet away, and to the east, a dirt county road and our neighbors' houses in the distance, but also the sunrise. When I sit anywhere upstairs, I can look out windows to the east, south, and west, all at the same time, and all I see is open countryside and the sky. I see trees, birds, wildlife, our horses grazing in the pasture. I feel surrounded by the outdoors, and although our house size is much smaller, it feels much larger and open. My wife and I have discussed the effect that living in these two different places, only four miles apart, has had on us. Even though our barn home is much smaller, we both have the feeling of being freer, more open, and more in tune with nature. I spend more time reading and writing. I feel more open and expansive. We didn't do anything drastic, like move to a different country or different state. We only live four miles away, but changing houses has drastically affected the being that I am. Like a deserted beach has a different vibration than a New York street, the barn home has a very different energetic vibration than the Craftsman home in town.

How small of a change in our environment can affect us as Beings? Any change in the environment can affect us as Beings. For example, imagine that you are working at home trying to get an important work project done in thirty minutes. Which environment would be more conducive to accomplishing this task?

Option one: sitting at the kitchen island while your significant other is preparing dinner and two children are running around the kitchen with the television blaring in the background.

Option two: sitting at your desk in your home study, door closed, quiet, with no distractions.

Taking this one step further, let's imagine a single room in your home: the kitchen. Does your kitchen feel different when everything is sparkling clean, all of the dishes are put away in the cupboards, the counters are clear, and everything is in the proper place compared to a sink full of dishes, dirty counters, and plates and glasses cluttering the island? This is the same room with all of the same objects, but the environment and vibration feel very different.

Most Beings never consider the effect the environment has on them as Beings. The environment is a variable a Being can control in the Being Equation. Be aware of the energetic vibration of the environment and how it is affecting you as a Being. The spatial aspect and the duration in the environment are two critical variables to consider when understanding the effect within the Being Equation.

Throughout this discussion, I have been careful to use the word "things" to describe physical objects in the environment. Other Beings (human, animal, plant, and insect) are all part of the environment and have an energetic vibration and impact us as well. There will be further discussion of relationships in a later chapter, but please understand that the presence or absence of other Beings in the environment can drastically change this variable in the Being Equation. For me, our dog Jessi always makes our house more energetically welcoming and comforting. The calm and restful environment of a tent in the woods can be completely transformed by a few mosquitos buzzing around the tent. A few plants scattered around an indoor space can change the environment from cold and stark to soft and inviting. Everything in the environment affects you as a Being. Understand this when choosing your environment.

PHYSICAL INPUTS

Think of Physical Inputs as anything a Being consumes that affects the mental or physical performance of the Being. An Input can be food, prescription drugs, supplements, water, alcohol, smells, psychedelics, and even the air one breathes. If it can be ingested, absorbed, or applied, it is a physical Input. Physical Inputs are important because they affect how a Being feels, physically and mentally, and affect how a Being interacts with the environment and other Beings. A Being has to consider all Physical Inputs transformed into the Physical Being they have been and are becoming to the answer the question: *who am I?* Think of everything you have physically consumed over your lifetime to fuel the Being that you are—each one of those Inputs has affected and created the Being that you are today.

The food we eat and the beverages we drink are fuel for our Physical Bodies and affect how we show up each day physically and energetically as Beings. We feel different mentally and physically when eating a healthy, nutritious diet versus eating fast food and getting drunk every night. A physically healthy Being is different when that same Being is drunk or hungover. On an immediate level, the sources you use to fuel your body on a day-to-day, hour-to-hour basis have a major impact on how you show up in the world. And 99 percent of us take this for granted.

There is a reason that top athletes follow a very specific food intake regime. They know it has a direct effect on their performance. It is the same for every single one of us. The difference is most of us don't pay attention to it because we do not think about performing at a high level day in and day out. We are not in a competition, and no one is keeping score, so why focus so strongly on diet, on the Inputs? Fair enough. I am the first to admit that I have made and continue to make food and beverage choices that are not optimal to my showing up fully in my day-to-day life, but why is that the case? The truth is that everything you take into your body as fuel directly impacts, positively or negatively, your ability to show up in the world. Most of us, including me, don't want to admit that because it means that the decisions I make about what to put into my body have consequences for those around me. I will not tell you what choices you should make regarding the Physical Inputs you use to fuel your body, mind, and Spirit, but I will ask you to consider this truth:

The choices you make regarding the Physical Inputs that are the fuel for your body, mind, and Spirit have consequences for you and those around you.

Many of us will say that when we make decisions about what we consume that we are not hurting anyone else. We will argue that it's only our body, our mind, and our Spirit that we impact, and we are not impacting others. This is not true. Do you show up better in the world when you have been eating a healthy diet and getting plenty of rest or when you are hungover and chowing down on fast food? Which "you" do your loved ones deserve? Which "you" does the world deserve to see? Which "you" do *you* deserve?

Even as I write these words, I don't necessarily want to hear them myself. Most of us don't want to admit this is true, but it is absolutely true. I am not going to tell you what diet or which choice is right for you. You already know. You have always known. The tough bit now is honoring that truth so you can show up fully for yourself and those around you.

QUESTIONS TO CONSIDER

- Does the city you live in support who you are as a Being?
- Does the country you live in support who you are as a Being?
- Does the house you live in support who you are as a Being?
- Are the Inputs you choose allowing the best *you* to show up?

CHAPTER 6

LIFE EVENTS

$$B_x(t) = f(SPIL_xE_x)$$

L_x = Life Events

Although this chapter will primarily be a description and discussion of Life Events and their role in the Being Equation, it will also introduce the variable of Egoic Interpretation. Chapter 7 will then cover Egoic Interpretation in depth, but the need to bring Egoic Interpretation into the chapter on Life Events highlights an important point about these two variables. They are deeply intertwined. They go together like peas and carrots, Bert and Ernie, Fred Astaire and Ginger Rogers, Brooks and Dunn, Romeo and Juliet. You get the picture. It is hard to discuss one without the other, and you can't have one without the other.

A Life Event can be thought of as anything that happened to you and that left a memory, conscious and/or subconscious. One could argue, correctly so, that under that definition, everything that has ever happened to you is a Life Event. This is true, and at this point, we could delve into an esoteric conversation about where "life" begins and where one event ends and another begins. And discuss if past Life Events exist and/or how the Life Events of your ancestors may affect you. I will unabashedly state right up front that I don't have definitive or authoritative answers to many of these questions regarding past lives or the exact moment of life beginning.

However, to understand Life Events in the context of the Being Equation, a logical leap is needed that may initially seem esoteric and hard to accept, but it is necessary. All Life Events are neutral. Imagine the perspective of a third person, an unbiased observer. An event happens, neither good nor bad, positive or negative; it just happens. Imagine that you are a video camera, recording every sight, sound, and detail that happens with zero emotional attachment to the event. Imagine that you are a little observer, seeing through the eyes, hearing through the ears, smelling through the nose, and touching through the skin, but you have zero emotional connection or reaction to what is being observed. What you are experiencing is a continuous flow of Life Events.

Our thoughts, feelings, and emotions arise from our Egoic Interpretation of Life Events. Things that happen, Life Events, have no meaning, no charge, and no feeling by themselves. Life Events only have meaning through Egoic Interpretation. Understanding Egoic Interpretation and the power it has on you as a Being is critical. We dive into Egoic Interpretation in much more detail in the coming chapters, but this is a critical concept to understand, and it can initially be unsettling when one first starts to contemplate it. I had never heard of this concept until I was in my mid-thirties, and it was completely eye-opening for me, but it can be overwhelming, so have patience with yourself and revisit this discussion as often as necessary.

ILLUSTRATING PERSPECTIVE

For me, understanding that Life Events are neutral and it is our Egoic Interpretation of the Life Event that applies the positive or negative, good or bad moniker to it, came down to the concept of perspective. To illustrate perspective, let's start by looking at the following examples:

Imagine there is a large stack of money on the table in front of you that totals one million dollars. It represents all of the money you have in the world. What was your reaction to the idea of one million dollars being all the money you had in the world? One million dollars is a large sum of money for most people. Most people would be ecstatic if they had one million dollars. Would you think, *Wow, one million dollars, I am rich!*? Let's talk about one million dollars from two different perspectives.

First, imagine that you live paycheck to paycheck. You barely keep the bills paid each month and have no money in savings. One million dollars represents a huge, amazing sum of money that would change your life.

Now, imagine that you are Oprah Winfrey, Warren Buffet, or Bill Gates. Your net worth had been measured in billions of dollars. Sitting before you, this one million in cash represents all of the money you have left in the world. All the rest of it is gone, and now you have only one million dollars.

Both scenarios contain the exact same one million dollars in cash sitting on the table before you, but can you imagine how you would feel differently about that one million dollars in each scenario?

This is perspective. In one case, you went from living paycheck to paycheck to having a huge sum of money. Many of your financial stresses and concerns are alleviated. You can breathe a sigh of relief. In fact, you may be elated. In the second scenario, you have lost billions of dollars. You now have huge money concerns, and one million dollars represents scraping the bottom of your financial barrel. How could this have happened?

Since this point on perspective is critical, let's look at one more example. Imagine that you go to a friend's house for dinner. You are seated at the table, ready to eat, and your friend serves you a glass of water, a few slices of bread, and a small chunk of cheese. Now, let's envision two different scenarios that create two different perspectives.

Scenario one: You have been hard at work all day and have been looking forward to this dinner with a friend. Your friend is a great cook, and in the past, the meals at his house have been fun affairs filled with great food and wine. You always look forward to these meals and even intentionally had a small lunch so you would have plenty of room to eat lots of great food and drink plenty of wine.

Scenario two: You have been stuck on a small, deserted island for three days. There was no food or fresh water. You are starving, dehydrated, and delirious. You are sunburned, and your head aches from dehydration. You have been dreaming about the cold, refreshing feeling of water.

How do you think you would react in each scenario seeing the food and water placed before you? Would you feel disappointed or grateful? Remember, same bread, same cheese, same water. Nothing has changed except perspective.

These two scenarios represent extreme examples of perspective, but realize that everything that happens to us is exactly like this. We filter every Life Event through the lens of perspective. This is typically done at the subconscious level. We do not consciously pause and ask, *What is my perspective on this situation?* We are not even consciously aware that we are assigning positive or negative, good or bad, to every Life Event. It just happens, and we accept it as our reality. Once we are aware of perspective, it can become a very powerful tool in the variable of Egoic Interpretation.

To explore perspective further, let's look at a simple scenario from four different perspectives, and see how each Being in the scenario has a different interpretation of events based on their perspective.

THE FABLE OF THE FOUR BEINGS

Let's imagine an event involving four Beings: two flies, a dog, and a human...humor me.

A dog is sleeping in his dog bed, directly under a table. Two flies are on the table, nibbling on a crumb of food. A human walks in with a fly swatter and whacks at the flies, killing one while the other flies away. The memories of each of the Beings may be as follows:

The Dog: I was startled awake by the human whacking with a stick thing on top of the table.

Live Fly: Dead Fly and I were eating when something big came towards us. The big thing got close, swung something towards us, it made a loud noise, and I flew. When I circled back, my friend was dead on the table.

Dead Fly: Live Fly and I were eating when something big came towards us. The big thing got close, swung something, and the lights went out for good.

The Human: I walked into the room with a fly swatter in my hand. I saw two flies on the table. I killed one, and one got away. I woke up the dog when I hit the table with the fly swatter.

Now, the (imagined) perspective from each Being:

The Dog: Why is it that every time I fall asleep under the table, the human walks in here and slams something on top to scare me? I wish he would stop doing that. I don't bother him when he is sleeping. (Notice, there is no knowledge of the flies that are the cause of the human's behavior.)

Live Fly: I must be careful when I see another one of those big things with a stick. I was eating with Dead Fly, and that big thing killed Dead Fly.

Dead Fly: No perspective (which in itself could be a cause for debate amongst some who believe in a specific type of afterlife).

The Human: Flies are dirty. If they are outside, that is fine, but if they bring their dirt and germs into my house, they deserve to die.

Here is where it *really* gets juicy.

As I have tried to show, our perspective is not always, in fact, hardly ever, an exact unbiased, "just the facts," recollection of what happens.

Whether we consciously know it or not, our perspective is biased by the stories we already have in our heads. Our brains often change, bend, and/or warp reality in an effort to protect us or make reality fit the stories we already believe about how things are or how things should be. This often happens at a subconscious level for lots of different reasons. The way to check your perspective for accuracy is to move it from the subconscious to conscious with one simple yet incredibly powerful question. Grab your highlighter, write this in your journal, tattoo this on your forearm. This is a question that can literally change your life: *what Story am I telling myself?*

WHAT STORY AM I TELLING MYSELF?

We will discuss the concept of Story in more detail in later chapters, but for now, *Story* can be thought of as the view or understanding a Being has about the world and how they exist in it. Perspective plays a major role in generating the stories we tell ourselves. Let's go back to the human's Story about the fly encounter. There is an infinite number of stories the human could be telling themselves about flies. These stories are a combination of only two things: what that human has been told about flies by other humans and what that human has personally observed of flies.

For fun, how many stories can we make up about flies right now?

1. My mom told me flies are dirty. All they do is carry disease and poop every time they land on something. They should all be killed.
2. Flies are important pollinators of plant species and are extremely beneficial to ecosystems.
3. Flies are excellent at cleaning up all the leftover food crumbs we leave around the house.

4. Flies serve no purpose in the world other than to buzz around and irritate people.
5. Flies have incredibly developed eyesight. Their ocular system is an incredible feat of nature and design. They should be admired.
6. Flies are so cool. I have a fly tattoo! How could you ever kill a fly?
7. Flies like poop. How do they always find the poop?
8. Flies are amazing because they start as maggots, crawling around, and then they turn into something that can fly. That is so much cooler than going from crawling to walking like humans.

What if the human in our example had been raised by parents who were entomologists that specialized in the study of Musca domestica, the genus and species of the house fly, and had passed on their love and knowledge of all house flies to the human? Let's say that this particular human grew up in a house adorned with books, posters, and abstract artwork and long dinner debates on the classification, merits, and misunderstood greatness of the genus Musca. Thanks to his parents' love of all things Musca, this human knows as much or more about flies, including the miraculous physiology of their compound eyes, the diversity of regions they inhabit, and all the ecosystem benefits they provide. Unfortunately, this particular human does not have happy memories of childhood because his parents seemed to be far more interested in flies than they were in human beings. Now, every time this human sees a fly, a mighty member of Musca, he thinks of his unhappy childhood and how he blames clan Musca and wants to kill every single one he sees.

The point here is that the Story we tell ourselves about any situation is heavily influenced by all of the past events and the stories we have told ourselves around those events. These all add up to form our Egoic Interpretation of the Life Event as it occurs in the present moment. You see, each Life Event has an associated Egoic Interpretation.

INTRODUCING THE EGOIC INTERPRETATION

The Egoic Interpretation can be defined as the combination of thoughts, feelings, and emotions, both conscious and subconscious, associated with any given Life Event.

There is an individual Egoic Interpretation associated with each Life Event because that is the way the system works. A Life Event occurs. And based on our past experience, which includes all previous Life Events and Egoic Interpretations, we view the Life Event from a particular perspective. Based on our perspective in that given moment in time, while the Life Event is occurring and we are running the experience through the conscious and subconscious portions of our brain, we rapidly create an Egoic Interpretation of the Life Event. The Egoic Interpretation of a Life Event in the present moment can be changing in the present moment as the event is occurring. Imagine this as a real-time, moving needle. As long as one is thinking about or experiencing the Life Event, either consciously or subconsciously, that little needle is moving, and the value has the potential to change. At some point, the particular Life Event moves from the present moment into the past. Since we are using an equation that includes time, (t), we can think of each Life Event in discrete time, meaning each Life Event has a discrete beginning and end.

In order to understand the timeline of a Life Event, it may help to think of a sporting event. A typical sporting event has a distinct starting point and a distinct end point. Everything that happens between the starting and end points is part of the event. The same goes for Life Events. Think of a Life Event moving into the present moment the same as the start of a sporting event. Once the sporting event begins, everyone is in the stadium until the final buzzer. The final buzzer of the sporting event is the equivalent of the Life Event moving from the present moment into the past. Life Events are each their own moment. For example, someone may think of their divorce process as one Life Event that lasted for a year. That would be incorrect. The divorce was actually a series of thousands of individual Life Events that occurred interspersed with millions of non-related-to-divorce Life Events that happened over the course of the year. The brain likes to sort, classify, organize, and lump all of the related Life Events together to save bandwidth, but this categorization is not accurate. Each Life Event occurs discreetly in its own present moment.

Our conscious brain only has so much attention and bandwidth to apply to anything occurring in the present moment, and at some point, it switches to consciously focusing on something else. Our subconscious brain continues to record information, but we are no longer consciously aware of this information. Now, remember that needle I referenced earlier? When we are in the present moment of a Life Event, that little needle is moving just like the needle in an EKG monitor. When the end of the game occurs, meaning the Life Event moves from present moment to past and from our conscious awareness, wherever that needle ends up is the value of the Egoic Interpretation that is associated with that Life Event. That value will remain associated with that Life Event and will not change until the Life Event is brought back into conscious awareness, into the present moment. Then, the associated Egoic Interpretation that is attached can be reviewed by our conscious mind. We will decide if we still hold the same Egoic Interpretation or if it needs to be changed. If we never consciously think of the Egoic Interpretation, then it remains at the value originally assigned. This may sound complicated, but let me give you a real-world example.

I remember drinking some cold coffee when I was around five. My mom had a cup sitting on her desk, and I asked if I could taste it. She let me, and I remember that it was terrible. It was cold and bitter. The taste stayed in my mouth for hours, and starting at that point, I really disliked coffee. For the next twenty-five years, I did not drink coffee, and yet every time someone would ask me if I like coffee, I immediately responded, "No." I would not even give it a try. The Life Event of tasting coffee occurred when I was five years old, and yet every time coffee was offered, I immediately responded, "No." I did not consciously access the entire memory of the Life Event of tasting coffee. I did not have to spend the energy and conscious bandwidth diving back into my past, accessing, and remembering the entire memory to make a decision on whether I liked coffee. I had a short, easy, subconscious default of "no to coffee." This default value for coffee was my Egoic Interpretation.

Then, when I was around thirty, I was very tired at work, and I had a big project I needed to complete. Everyone in the office regularly drank coffee and talked about how it gave them energy and focus. I needed to get focused and get the project done, so I decided to give coffee another try. I made myself a cup, took a sip, and really enjoyed it. I liked the aroma and flavor, and within a few minutes, I was feeling energized and focused. Now I had a new Life Event and associated Egoic Interpretation for that Life Event. Fifteen years later, I enjoy coffee every day. I also have a new perspective to apply to the Life Event of my five-year-old experience with coffee, which we will discuss in later chapters.

This information regarding coffee was always there but would only be accessed consciously when something in the present moment made me think of coffee. All Life Events are the same, always there but only consciously accessed when something in the present moment pulls them into consciousness. Their relationship to the subconscious is a whole different story, however. Understanding how Life Events, perspective, Egoic Interpretation, conscious, and subconscious interact in relation to the past, present, and future is at the crux of moving to answer the question: *who am I?* Stay with me here. It sounds complicated, but the next few chapters will be a lot of fun. You are about to see how deep the rabbit hole gets, and you may be surprised to find out it is also much simpler than you think.

THE BRAIN

We can't go much further without discussing "the brain."

I have used a number of brain-related terms, including conscious and subconscious (some people use unconscious, but that always makes me think of a knocked-out boxer). Scientists and others believe that everything that has ever happened to you, including events that you do not consciously remember, is stored within your subconscious mind. It would therefore make sense that these Life Events affect you even though you are not consciously aware of them. We are all familiar with these types of memories; when a friend or family member or a smell reminds us of someone or something we hadn't thought of for twenty years, it all comes flooding back. We could not have willfully pulled that memory forward if we had wanted, but one gentle prod of the grey matter from an outside source reminds us.

To understand how this happens, we have to understand how the brain works. Even though we think of our brain as a single organ, it is actually a series of systems cobbled together over a long period of time. Let's use the human body as an analogy. We use the word "body" to describe the entirety of our physical form. When we use the word "body," we all have a general understanding that the human body, in most cases, consists of a series of unique parts, including arms, legs, head, feet, hands, torso, etc.

Humans have the default knowledge that a body is composed of parts. We also think of animal, insect, and plant bodies as composed of a series of parts. However, when it comes to the brain or "mind," we think of it as one big whole. Unless you are a neurologist or particularly interested in the brain, you think of the brain as one uniform body part. In this analogy, the word brain would be equivalent to the word body. In fact, the brain is composed of a series of parts, like the pieces of a body that all work together but have distinctive functions and purposes. The brain is an amazing, beautiful, and complex symphony that we don't even fully understand, nor have we been able to create anything externally with its complex computational power.

At our current level of understanding, we believe that different parts of the brain developed over time, with the earliest parts of the brain, the limbic brain, being the fight-or-flight system designed to quickly recognize threats, take charge, and do what is necessary to keep us alive. There are also parts of the brain designed for higher-order thinking and complex thought. For doing things like writing, creating, and solving. The types of things you think about only *after* your basic needs—food, shelter, water, and safety—are met.

Different parts of your brain are in charge during different situations; we do not consciously choose or control which parts are working. We can try to train and prepare our brains for different events and activities, but ultimately, we can't control the parts of our brain like we control the parts of our body. However, we do have some ways to control certain aspects of how we interact with our brain, specifically how we interact with memory.

For the purposes of this discussion, I am going to switch from separating the brain into its physical components and instead divide it into a conscious portion and a subconscious portion. The conscious portion is everything we can access at will and the portion we can actively focus and use. The subconscious portion of our brain is the giant storehouse of information and also where the automatic controls live, controls like our autonomic nervous system. Even though we are talking about them separately, there is also a tremendous amount of communication back and forth between the two. A commonly used analogy to represent these two portions of the brain is a computer. If our brain was a computer, then the RAM portion, random access memory, would be the conscious mind, and the ROM, or read-only memory, would be the subconscious.

The RAM, or conscious portion, is the part that we generally control. It is what we can focus and utilize to accomplish certain tasks. The ROM portion is much larger, orders of magnitude larger, and this is where every detail of everything that has ever happened to us is stored. The thing about this memory and brainpower is that we have much less control and much less understanding about how it all works. Just like a computer, there is an interface between our RAM and our ROM, or our conscious and our subconscious, and that interface is where it gets really, really interesting.

The interface is not something that many people even think about because it appears without our even being aware of it, but I believe understanding this interface is a critical component to defining your life and deciding how you want to live it. Although our conscious mind is amazing, it absolutely pales in comparison to the raw computational and memory power of our subconscious mind. That said, from a practical standpoint, our subconscious mind is rather powerless without the actions of the conscious mind. They need each other. There is a saying that knowledge is power. Knowledge, by itself, is not power. *Knowledge, by itself, is useless. Knowledge, when used to inform action, is power.*

Think of the subconscious mind as the storehouse of all the information that has ever come to you. The conscious mind does not have the bandwidth to deal with all the information coming through all our senses and feeding it back out to all our past experiences that may have a bearing on a current situation, so the conscious mind establishes a series of rules or protocols to prioritize and categorize all the information coming through it at any given time. Most people are not even aware that the conscious mind has established these protocols for them. They have become so ingrained that people think this is just how it is. They do not realize a choice has been made for them or that they have an ability to change that choice.

To emphasize this point, I would like to tell you the story of Daniel Kish. Daniel has been blind since he was very young, but he is able to navigate and describe his world through the use of sound. Daniel is one of the world's foremost experts on and practitioners of human echolocation. He uses a series of clicks he creates with his mouth and the reverberations he receives back from them to get a picture of the world around him. Daniel independently developed this skill and practice as a young boy. Studies have shown that those who use human sonar, aka echolocation, as a primary means of navigation, are activating the "visual system" of the brain when processing the information they receive from clicking to get a visual picture of their surroundings. They have a 3D perspective of space. There is depth, structure, and dimension. There is also a sense of texture, of whether surfaces are hard or soft.

Daniel, and other human echolocators, do not possess any special or advanced hearing attributes. Nothing greater than you or I possess. In fact, with enough training, we all could likely be taught the skills of echolocation. The difference is that Daniel has made the conscious decision that all of the bits of sound coming to him are important, and he has prioritized his conscious mind to focus on that information. His visual impairment means that he does not have visual information competing for bandwidth. I haven't spoken directly to Daniel, but I would guess that he does not have to consciously choose every day to prioritize the auditory information. Over time, this has become his dominant, default program, just as those of us who can see have vision as our default program. Our conscious mind does this defaulting because it is always trying to save bandwidth, retaining it for whatever new thing/threat/need might arise in our environment. Our conscious mind does not have the capacity to deal with all sensory Inputs at once, at least not without a *lot* of training and focus, so it develops these defaults over time, and soon we are no longer aware that we are making choices based on subconscious information. *Changing your life is all about understanding your defaults and deciding if those defaults are still serving you.*

Let me give you a practical example of your conscious mind's ability to deal with a maximum amount of sensory Inputs. One day, I was driving down the highway to my office as I had done hundreds of times before. As I was driving, I received a phone call, and using the car's hands-free calling system, I answered the call and began a conversation. The conversation was an intense one, and it required me to focus my attention and thought on what the other person was saying and how I was going to respond. This conversation only lasted ten minutes, but when I hung up the phone, I realized that I had driven three miles past my exit for work. I had not even realized I had passed my exit. I am embarrassed to say that during the conversation, I was no longer even consciously aware of my destination. I was just driving. Keeping the car in my lane and avoiding other cars. It was like I was on autopilot.

Truthfully, a discussion of the brain and how it works deserves multiple books itself. Scientists still do not fully understand how it works.

Let's summarize the key takeaways we need to understand moving forward:

1. The active functioning of the brain can be divided into two broad, functional categories: conscious and subconscious.
2. The conscious brain is the portion each of us actively controls and focuses. It is orders of magnitude smaller than our subconscious portion in terms of computing power (RAM).
3. The conscious brain has a maximum bandwidth of the amount of information it can process at any one time.
4. The subconscious brain is the portion of the brain you do not actively control.
5. The subconscious brain (ROM) is orders of magnitude larger in computing power than the conscious brain (RAM).
6. Everything we experience, whether consciously or subconsciously, is stored in our subconscious.
7. We cannot always willfully access all of the information stored in our subconscious.

The distinction between conscious and subconscious and how they interact is critical, so I would like to give you another analogy to help clarify the concept.

LIFE EVENTS AND THEIR CRATES

The last scene of *Indiana Jones and the Raiders of the Lost Ark* shows a large wooden crate containing the Ark of the Covenant being wheeled into an enormous, dimly lit warehouse filled with rows and rows of crates stacked from floor to ceiling for as far as the eye can see. The non-descript wooden crates are all shapes and sizes, and one could imagine walking down rows and aisles for days and weeks and not being able to tell one row from the next. This is how I picture my subconscious mind. It is a giant storehouse of information. Every

Life Event, everything I have ever experienced, is stacked in a crate in one of these never-ending aisles. Some crates are covered in dust and haven't been touched for decades, but there the crate sits, available if needed. I think of my conscious mind as the person that has been working in the warehouse since the warehouse opened. This person knows their way around the warehouse and has a good idea of what is in many of the crates, but there are some of which this person has no content knowledge. New crates keep showing up and getting stored away, but this warehouse worker can only deal with so many crates at once. As a result, there are crates they have never opened.

Each crate is a Life Event. The conscious mind is the warehouse worker that can run around and find crates when requested, but it is impossible to know about every crate. They do their best, but sometimes they stumble upon crates they didn't know about. Often crates get lost. Some people spend lots of time in their warehouse, trying to keep it organized, trying to be cognizant of each new crate going in. Other people are aware that crates are going into the warehouse but have no idea how many are coming in or what is necessarily in them. They show up at the warehouse, punch the time clock, and put in their eight hours. Later, we will discuss tools you can use to organize and use your warehouse more effectively. For now, know that everything that happens, in every moment, is going in your warehouse, whether you realize it or not.

In this analogy, the warehouse represents what we are storing in our subconscious about the past. The crates coming into the warehouse door represent the present moment, and everything on the outside of the warehouse is future. The warehouse worker is our conscious mind. I like to consider how I am using the warehouse worker at any given point in time.

Mindfulness has become a more prevalent concept over the last few years. I think of mindfulness as bringing the focus of your conscious mind into the present moment and focusing awareness on the information coming to you through your senses and thoughts in the moment. For me, this would be like the warehouse worker standing right in the doors of the warehouse, carefully watching what is being packed into each crate and then deciding where in the warehouse each crate should be stored. This sounds great, but in reality, the warehouse worker also has other things to do, and it is nearly impossible for them to stand at the door watching crates as they come in. The crates are constantly coming, twenty-four hours a day, seven days a week, 365 days a year for your entire life.

Not only does the warehouse worker have to pay attention to the crates coming in, but sometimes there is a request to retrieve a crate containing something that happened in the past, or maybe even a bunch of crates, so they have to leave the warehouse doors, go find the requested crates and bring them back to the front of the warehouse. This occurs when we use our conscious mind to try and recall a memory from the past. Other times, the warehouse worker has to write reports on the contents of future crates. This requires taking stock of related crates from the past and then guessing what may be in the future crates. Again, when this is happening, new crates are still rolling in the door.

This warehouse analogy shows us why so much focus has been placed on teaching us to be in the present moment. When we are feeling scattered and distracted, it is like we are asking our warehouse worker to run in ten different directions. Crates are coming in, requests are flying around for old crates, and reports are due on what crates might be coming in next week. The warehouse worker has no idea where to start and is turning in circles. Does this sound familiar? A simple way to think of mindfulness is: being very direct about what you want your warehouse worker to do at a given moment. I personally do not believe your warehouse worker can multitask. They might be able to switch back and forth between tasks quickly, but they cannot do multiple tasks at once. Mindfulness is simply consciously deciding which task you want the warehouse worker to do.

If we go back to my story about missing my work exit due to a phone call, we can see that my warehouse worker was being pulled in too many directions. I asked him to go grab some crates from the past regarding the person who was on the phone, then to analyze the contents of the crates to predict what crates may be coming in the future. While this was happening, a few crates snuck through the warehouse door without my warehouse worker seeing them.

To further add to this analogy, each crate has an Egoic Interpretation value associated with it. I think of this as a piece of paper right on top of the contents of the crate. You pop the crate open, and the first thing you see is that piece of paper with the Egoic Interpretation on it. The paper has been right there since the crate was packed away.

We started the chapter by introducing Life Events, which we learned are neutral by their very nature. It is through the application of perspective, in combination with the relevant stories we have built around a given scenario, that we create an Egoic Interpretation of that Life Event moving forward. We then file that Life Event away in the warehouse of our mind with its associated Egoic Interpretation. This Life Event and Egoic Interpretation then go into the mix to create the Story we have around this topic moving forward.

In the next chapter, we will continue to explore how these variables interact to form a Story and feed our future Egoic Interpretations.

QUESTIONS TO CONSIDER

Have you ever considered the concept that all Life Events are neutral and it is through perspective and Egoic Interpretation that we assign a value to them?

Can you think of a Life Event where your default is based on an experience from a long time ago (like the coffee example)?

Are you making conscious choices on how you're allocating the time of your warehouse worker?

CHAPTER 7

EGOIC INTERPRETATION

$$B_x(t) = f(SPIL_xE_x)$$

E_x = Egoic Interpretation

In Chapter 6, we defined Egoic Interpretation as the combination of thoughts, feelings, and emotions, both conscious and subconscious, associated with any given Life Event. The Egoic Interpretation is the value that our conscious mind assigns to any Life Event while it is occurring or once it has occurred.

The value of E_x assigned to the Life Event at the present moment is based on everything that has occurred in your life up to the present moment. Everything the Being Equation represents up until the exact present moment creates the E_x for that Life Event. This sounds complex, but when thought of on the practical level, it makes sense. Let's work through an example to see how the different variables in the Being Equation act to create the Egoic Interpretation of a Life Event in the present moment. This is important because once you understand this concept, you can consciously make decisions to create the opportunity for the best possible Egoic Interpretation of a Life Event in real time.

EGOIC INTERPRETATION IN CONTEXT

Here is an example from my life. I have never been good at putting away my clean laundry. Sometimes my wife will do the laundry, or I will do the laundry, fold it, and then leave it sitting on the couch or bed for days. I am not proud of this trait, but it happens regularly. The following scenario has played out in our household many times.

My wife: "Erik, that clean laundry has been sitting there for three days. Do you think you could put it away?"

Me, with a bit of shame and slight annoyance for being asked to put it away: "Sure, sorry I haven't put my laundry away. I keep forgetting to do it."

My wife: "How can you forget? You have walked past it at least twenty times in the past three days."

At this point, I would like you to think of this dialogue exchange as happening in two different contexts, so we can compare and contrast different variables and see how they can change. Each context is very basic, and the assumptions we make about the five variables are going to be generalities.

Context one: I have spent a relaxing day at home. My wife, Christi, and I had a nice, healthy lunch together, and I have just come back from a walk around the lake with our dog, Jessi.

Context two: I have just walked in the door at the end of a very long workday. I haven't eaten anything all day, and I just sat down in the chair, cracked open a beer, and turned on the television so I can turn off my brain and unwind a bit.

Spirit: In context one, my Spiritual energy has been recharged from going for a walk in nature and having a relaxing day. In context two, my Spiritual energy is likely depleted from a long, stressful day at work with no quiet time for myself.

Physical Body: One could argue that this variable could be the same for both scenarios as it relates to my genetics, and it may be. However, some epigenetic changes could have occurred with me spending time in a natural environment versus an office environment. One could argue that the office environment creates an elevated sense of stress, which could be activating certain biological pathways depending on my epigenetic predispositions to certain stressors. I will leave it up to you on the specifics, but I think we can agree that our physiology is different in these two contexts.

Inputs/Environment: In context one, I am relaxed and have recently eaten a healthy meal. My body is well fueled, and the natural setting has been a soothing environment. In context two, I have been in an office all day and have just walked in the door. I am in front of the television, and my only nutrition for the past eight hours is the two sips of beer I have taken. I am hungry and tired and definitely a grouch.

Life Events: For the purposes of this exercise, let's assume for both contexts, I have had all of the same previous Life Events, and those Life Events are as follows. As I mentioned, my mom used to constantly remind me, push me, scold me, to put my clothes away. Christi and I have been married for over twenty years, and she has had similar frustrations.

Egoic Interpretation: In both contexts, let's assume my Egoic Interpretations of all past Life Events related to putting away my laundry are the same.

Now, let's pick it back up in real-time and see how the Egoic Interpretation of this event can be changed based on the impact of the other four variables in the Being Equation.

Remember, here is the dialogue again:

My wife: "Erik, that clean laundry has been sitting there for three days. Do you think you could put it away?"

Me, with a bit of shame and slight annoyance for being asked to put it away: "Sure, sorry I haven't put my laundry away. I keep forgetting to do it."

My wife: "How can you forget? You have walked past it at least twenty times in the past three days."

Context one: I am calm and relaxed from the walk, and I think to myself, *You know, she is right. I have no excuse. Why do I have such a hard time with laundry?* I think back to all those times my mom had to remind and cajole me and threaten me with punishment for not putting away my laundry. Why was that?

And then I start to think about how my mom must have felt having to do that. She was working her tail off as a single mother, feeding me, and doing all of the laundry herself, and I didn't even have the courtesy to thank her for washing and folding my laundry. It must have made her feel really unappreciated when she saw my laundry that she had washed and folded, lying in a pile on the floor beside my bed. That was insensitive of me.

Then I think how it must make Christi feel to have spent time washing and folding laundry and then for me not to do her the courtesy of putting it away. Or what kind of respect am I showing myself by not putting away the laundry I wash and fold?

With all of this in mind, I respond in the following manner:

Me: "You know, you are right. I just realized that not putting away my laundry is disrespectful to you. I am sorry. I will put it away now, and it is something I would like you to make me aware of in the future if I don't put it away in a timely manner. Thank you."

In context one, not only have I changed my Egoic Interpretation of this Life Event, but I have consciously gone back and quickly realized that all of the previous Egoic Interpretations of "laundry events," where I was feeling annoyed and nagged about putting away my laundry, were actually me being ungrateful and unappreciative. I make a mental note to really spend time looking at this and thinking about how I can change my Story around laundry going forward. I can do this because, in context one, the other variables in the Being Equation were in a positive space and positioned me for a positive outcome.

Now, let's rewind the tape and look at this scenario as it plays out in context two:

Context two: I am tired, grouchy, and mentally and emotionally checked out. I think to myself, *Is she serious? I just walked in the door from a long day at work, I haven't eaten a thing, I am trying to unwind for a few minutes and have a beer, and she is going to hit me with this laundry thing. Again? Seriously?*

And then I say: "I don't know why I forgot to put it away. Your work stuff has been sitting over there for the past three days, but you haven't put it away either."

Do I need to go any further here for you to realize how this plays out? My Spiritual energy was low, my Inputs were in a negative space, and the response I gave is sure to create another negative Egoic Interpretation to add to the growing collection of negative laundry Egoic Interpretations. Please notice that this is the exact same Life Event, a few words back and forth over laundry, but the Being that I am reacts very differently in the moment depending on the other variables of Being Equation in that moment.

THE INTERCONNECTIVITY OF LIFE EVENTS

This may seem like an oversimplification of life, but it's not. Every single Life Event happens exactly in this manner, and you will be a different person in the moment, depending on where you stand on each of the other four variables in the moment. They are all interconnected.

As the Being Equation states, everything that has happened to a Being up until that exact moment in time affects the value of E_x for the Life Event because everything that has happened is represented by the Being Equation up to that exact moment in time. All of the variables are time-dependent and have the ability to change over time, and in some cases, to change rapidly over time.

From our laundry scenario, let's look at I_x, Inputs, for example. We saw that a healthy meal versus no food and a beer had a direct impact on the value of E_x. This change in Inputs, in I_x, resulted in a different value of E_x, and subsequently, the Being that I am moving forward. Simply put, a small change in any variable can create a change in the value of E_x at any moment.

A key to activating the power of the Being Equation is awareness. The idea of awareness leads to a larger point. Awareness is a superpower. If you would like, you can substitute the word mindfulness for awareness. Being mindful means being consciously aware. I think of awareness as simply bringing something into consciousness. Until something is in our consciousness, we have no power, on a conscious level, to react to it. However, once we are aware and the variable is in our consciousness, we can react.

And we decide how to react by being curious and asking questions. How does this make me feel? Do I want to feel this way? What belief or Story is making me feel this way in this situation? Do I still believe this belief? Is this belief still serving me? Should I change this belief? What in my past is causing me to have this belief? Is the Story for this situation still the same? Do I want to change the Story? And the questions go on and on.

The power of working through the Being Equation with another person, or a group of people, is that the others can make you consciously aware of things you were not conscious of before. There is an old saying that you cannot read the label if you are stuck inside the bottle. Sometimes you cannot see what would be completely obvious to someone outside of the situation. You can make a lot of progress with the Being Equation on your own, but there are times you absolutely need someone else to make you consciously aware of something you cannot see otherwise.

How does all of this create Story? The word Story is shorthand for the combination of the Life Event and the Egoic Interpretation of that Life Event. Those two variables interact to create our Story of what happened. Many people do not even realize they are telling themselves a Story about many of the events that happened in their lives. They believe their Story is the actual, unbiased account of the Life Event, no perception involved, just the facts, and this is where the danger lies. And often, we have stories stacked upon stories and don't even realize it.

EGO AND EGOIC INTERPRETATION

I would like to take a moment to draw a distinction between Egoic Interpretation and ego. Egoic Interpretation is the singular "value" our ego places on a Life Event. There is a one-to-one relationship between Egoic Interpretation and a Life Event. Your ego is responsible for creating the Story you tell yourself about any Life Event. In contrast, ego refers to a cumulative body that encompasses and is shaped by all our Life Events and their associated Egoic Interpretations up until the present moment. It can be useful to create an analogy of your ego and your Physical Body. Your Physical Body in the present moment is the sum total of everything you have consumed since the moment you were born up until this exact moment. It has been shaped by your history of movement and all of the Life Events that have affected your Physical Body up to this moment. Your Physical Body has wounds and scars that are markers of past traumas, and the level of physical fitness is the result of the care you have shown your body since the day you were born. Your ability to physically move and respond to your environment in this present moment is dependent on all the things that have happened to your body up until the present moment.

Your ego is much the same. Your ego, as a whole, is the sum total of every Life Event and the Egoic Interpretation of that Life Event you hold. In mathematical terms, ego is equal to: $(L_1E_1 + L_2E_2 + ... L_xE_x)$. Similar to your Physical Body, your ego has its wounds and scars. Just as your current physical shape is impacted by how much care and attention you have given your Physical Body, so is your ego dependent on the care and attention you have placed on it.

In this analogy, there is one big difference between ego and Physical Body. You cannot go back in time by ten years and start exercising to change the current condition of your Physical Body. However, in the present moment, you can go back to a Life Event that happened ten years ago and change the Egoic Interpretation of that Life Event, resulting in changing your ego in the present moment.

Wait, what?

Yes, you have the power right now. The Being Equation shows you exactly who you are. I am not saying that you can change the Life Event itself. That will never change. However, if it were something traumatic or caused resentment or anger, you could soften and change your Egoic Interpretation of the Life Event at this very moment.

There are some Beings who strive to have a complete dissolution of ego. I do not claim to know if this is possible. I do know from personal experience that you have the ability to change the Egoic Interpretation of any past Life Event, and the effects of doing this can be profound. I know that some reading this will be thinking, come on, can it really be that simple? *All you have to do is change the Egoic Interpretation of previous Life Events, and you can change your ego, thereby changing the very Being that you are?* Yes, it is. I battled this fact myself for a long time. I, just like many others, like to complicate things. I often think the answer can't be that simple. If it is simple, it must be wrong.

It *is* that simple. You do not need to complicate it any further. Why is this? Remember, every Life Event has an associated Egoic Interpretation. Think of the Egoic Interpretation for each Life Event as shorthand for how we "feel" about the Life Event. Our conscious brain is always trying to save time, so it uses the value of the Egoic Interpretation already assigned to the Life Event whenever that event is accessed, whether consciously or subconsciously. If you consciously bring the Life Event into your conscious awareness, then your ego in the present moment has the ability to assign a new Egoic Interpretation value to that specific Life Event.

This is the work of self-reflection or any activity in which you are going back into the past to address Life Events. If, through whatever means, you are able to change the value of your Egoic Interpretation of that Life Event for future reference, then you have changed. By definition, your ego has changed, and the Being that you are in the present moment has changed because of the change in value of the Egoic Interpretation of the past. This is it. This is the crux of understanding Egoic Interpretation and how you can use it to change the Being you are in the present moment. The really cool thing about this is that the impact of this type of change can be instantaneous and can rapidly ripple through other Egoic Interpretations of past Life Events. It is that simple. It is not always easy, though it can be. But it is always that simple.

TESTING EGOIC INTERPRETATION

Let's do an exercise to show how this concept works. Now that you have the laundry scenario as an example, can you think of something that has been an ongoing situation in your life for many years? Think of something that you continue to do that creates a negative feeling in your life or in your interactions with others. It helps if it is something that seems on the surface to be a small or simple task.

It could be something simple like always being the one to take out the trash, or maybe you always eat ice cream before bed and feel bad about doing it, or maybe you are always the one in the office who makes the coffee.

Now, get curious about the situation. What is my default Egoic Interpretation for this circumstance? In the laundry scenario, my default was that laundry was always a pain and a chore, a point of contention. Why is that? Can I change my perspective and see a positive? Can I look forward and have a new perspective when someone washes and folds my laundry in the future? Someone loves me and cares about me enough to wash and fold my laundry. That is a gift right there.

QUESTIONS TO CONSIDER

- What recurring Life Events, if any, create negative Egoic Interpretations?
- What recurring Life Events, if any, create positive Egoic Interpretations?
- What past Life Event makes you cringe when you look at its Egoic Interpretation?
- Can you look back at a Life Event and an Egoic Interpretation that occurred in the last twenty-four hours and see them differently?

PART 2

BEING

CHAPTER 8

CLARITY AND KNOWLEDGE

Now that you have been introduced to the five variables of the Being Equation, let's take some time to discuss a few additional concepts you will need to effectively apply the Being Equation in your life. Let's start with clarity.

CLARITY

Why is clarity important in the context of the Being Equation? The clarity that arises from *knowing* who you are acts as a magnifying glass that focuses the universe to help you achieve your goals. In fact, clarity is so important, that if I could have one superpower, it would be clarity: the ability to create crystal clear, pure, beautiful clarity for myself and for others. Clarity, some of you may be saying, is a pretty lame superpower wish. *What about invisibility or superhuman strength, or the ability to fly?* Those are extremely cool superpowers, but I am still going with clarity. Here's why:

Clarity is the secret sauce, the golden ticket, the master key.

Imagine for a minute what your life would be like if you had perfect clarity of purpose and intention for yourself. If you knew exactly who you were and exactly what you were meant to do in life and exactly how to do it—you wouldn't be reading this book. You wouldn't need to. Think of all the time you spend trying to get clear on what to do next (at home, at work) and thinking about how to best spend your time. I spent the first forty-two years of my life with no clarity. As Napoleon Hill would say, I was drifting. Drifting through life and beating myself up because I could not find my "passion." I had no clarity.

Imagine if you knew, with perfect clarity, your goals and intentions in life, why you wanted to achieve those goals, and the steps you needed to take to reach them. How amazing would that be? How unstoppable would you feel? How much worry and stress would be removed from your life?

Now, imagine if you could sit down with any person in the world and instantly provide that same level of clarity to them. How grateful do you think they would be to receive that clarity? If I had that superpower, I would call myself Captain Clarity—or maybe even Commander Clarity! Seriously, how many wasted lives—including stress, worry, and confusion—could you save by providing instant clarity to someone?

Clarity is a superpower, and sometimes we stumble upon it. Unfortunately, most of us get clarity about the wrong things. There are many great books and tools out there on how to gain clarity in life, how to get clear on your goals, and how to achieve those goals, but these resources don't teach you how to challenge the foundation on which your goals are built.

Your subconscious is filtering every nanobyte of information that comes in through your five senses, comparing it against all the previous knowledge and past experience, and then passing to your conscious only the pieces of the information it deems relevant.

We are all mighty creators, and the universe is always trying to serve us to reach our goals. It is through clarity of thought and desire that we focus the universe towards achieving our objectives. In essence, as creators, we *are* the magnifying glass that focuses the universe, so our power of focus comes through our clarity. The problem is that we often do not *know*, at our core, what we want.

HOW DO WE "KNOW"?

Knowledge: (n) facts, information, and skills acquired by a person through experience or education; the theoretical or practical understanding of a subject.

There are two types of knowledge: external and internal. All external knowledge originates from interaction with the external world.

All of the external knowledge you have is composed of two elements:

1. What you have been told about the subject by others.
2. What you have personally observed about the subject yourself.

These are the only two sources of external knowledge. Either someone told you something, or you personally experienced it yourself through your five senses. That is it.

As I have mentioned previously, I gain clarity through conversations with Source. Here is an excerpt of a conversation with Source exploring the origins of knowledge. This dialogue is taken directly from my journal.

Me: Source, can you tell me about knowledge and if my thinking on the two, external sources of knowledge and one internal source of knowledge is correct?

Source: Knowledge is an interesting and tricky thing to talk about because it is a word like "success." It can have different meanings to many different people, and everyone thinks they know what it means when they hear it. The way you are using the word "knowledge," it basically means things that you have the ability to know, when in actuality, what you think you know may not really be the case at all. Take, for example, the table your journal is sitting on while you write these words. You know this table is made of wood. You think you know what wood is. Wood is a material that comes from a tree. You may even get as specific as knowing what species of tree the wood comes from. So, you know that the table is made of part of a tree, but what is wood really? What are the actual particles and processes that make wood? What chemicals and materials are in the wood? Is it accurate to call it wood? Your knowledge is only to a certain level. A physicist may look at what you call wood and have entirely different knowledge and a different level of understanding than you do. A biologist, a materials scientist, a carpenter—all have different knowledge of what you call wood.

It is the same with everything. Each Being has a different knowledge of what something is. For example, a woodpecker doesn't see wood. It sees food or something that contains food. Most people never think of knowledge on this level. Everything you look at is the same. Out the window, you see an oak tree that was planted in honor of Christi's horse, Joshua. That tree has special meaning to you. Someone driving by sees a newly planted tree. A landscaper sees the tree as a Plains Oak tree, approximately twenty feet tall with a 2.5-inch diameter at breast height. It wholesales for $250 and would cost a customer $750 to have it installed. A biologist sees a member of the genus, Quercus, approximately seven years of age with a pinnacle growth form and an average life expectancy of 125–250 years. This particular species is known to be drought-tolerant and well-suited for the arid plains environment. The point is, if you asked all three of these Beings what that thing is outside the window, the response would be, "a tree," but each would have different knowledge. It is the same for every concept.

Me: Wow, I have never really thought of it that way, but that does make complete sense. So, this is the same for everything, not only physical objects. It seems that in order to have a coherent conversation or thought, especially involving more than one person, we need to be clear on what knowledge we assume we have, to become consciously aware of the origins of our knowledge, and to challenge whether that knowledge is something we still "believe."

Okay, but what about the second part? What about the internal source of knowledge?

Source: That one gets much trickier because it is not something tangible, nothing concrete that can be pointed to or measured. You will never be able to prove that it exists. I can tell even now there is part of you that is completely skeptical, and you are the one writing the book. This is faith. You either have faith that it exists or you don't, no two ways about it. Let me explain to you how these two concepts interact, and then you can think about it.

The external knowledge you have gained is all about how the external world works and how you fit into the world. It is about what society, family, and friends expect of you, how you move through society, and how you are expected to interact with the world. Even what you have learned about Spirituality, religions, and teachings that have come from outside of you about your inner world are external. The internal knowledge can only arise from within. Internal knowledge speaks in the language of feelings and intuition. Internal knowledge has none of the parameters of society or expectations. Internal knowledge cannot be quantified. Everyone has internal knowledge, but many people do not know what it is or have been trained by the external world not to listen to it.

CHAPTER 9

LOVE, ACCEPTANCE, AND FORGIVENESS

ACCEPTANCE

Acceptance is acknowledging the reality of the situation and being at peace with whatever you are acknowledging. I think of acceptance as a peaceful submission to the present reality. You no longer invest energy in wishing it was different, being angry about it, or hoping to change it. Your body, mind, and Spirit, your whole Being, realizes that it cannot be changed. Acceptance is liberating, freeing because no more energy or focus needs to be placed on that event. The event is not forgotten, but the emotional charge is removed, and it moves to the catalog of stored memory. It is there and can still be accessed.

We always think of acceptance in terms of the memories that are "bad," the ones that make us angry or sad or are traumatic, but there is a process for acceptance of "good" memories as well. It is nice to relive positive memories and look fondly back on events. This can be a great way to move into a positive energy space. The pitfall can happen when one spends too much time reliving the positive moments of the past and not being in the present. When the mind thinks the best has already happened and nothing as good can happen in the future. Reliving the feeling of passion when we were young and in love and putting our energy into the past experience, taking away the energy we could use to create that feeling in the present.

The most important acceptance we can practice is the acceptance of self. Accepting ourselves exactly as we are at this very moment. Lives have been destroyed, and are being destroyed, because we do not accept ourselves. We fight ourselves, beat ourselves up, fill our lives with "should haves," "would haves," and "could haves." The Being Equation is radical acceptance of the self because it states that you could be no other person and no other way in this present moment. Any Being would be exactly who you are now had they been born at the same time, to the same parents, and had exactly the same Inputs and Life Events as you. It could be no other way. Therefore, you can accept and fully embrace the good, the bad, and every aspect of you at this very present moment as exactly who you are.

The natural reaction to this knowledge is to say, but wait, if I had made some different choices, my life would be very different. This is true. The Being you are now is the sum total of all of your Life Events. If those Life Events would have been different, then you would be a different Being. If any variable had been different, you would be a different Being. A different choice at any Life Event would change who you are now. Remember, the Being Equation defines any Being at a point in time (t). Therefore, if you go back in time to the place in your life where you would have made a different choice, the Being Equation states that at that particular time (t), as the Being you were then, and given all of the Inputs you had at that given time, you would have made the exact choice that any Being would make had they been born at that exact time and with all the exact Inputs that you had up to that very moment in time. It could be no other way, and had you not made that choice, you would not be the Being you are right now at this time reading these words.

I want to make a very subtle but extremely critical distinction here. Please do not take this to mean that your life is pre-determined, that each choice is already decided. The Being Equation proves quite the opposite. In the present moment, you as a Being have complete choice. There is no pre-determination or destiny. The Being Equation states that whatever choice is made, the moment it moves from the present to the past, it becomes a choice that could have been no other way. All Inputs that happened to you as a Being led to you making that choice. Any other Being that had been born at the exact moment, at the exact location as you, to the exact same parents, and had all of the same Life Events up to that present moment, would have made the exact same choice. For this reason, you can radically accept yourself in this very moment because the Being you are now could have been no other way.

You cannot go back in time and change a choice that you made. That choice is locked in time. However, you can change the Story that you tell yourself, the Egoic Interpretation, around the choice, and you can act in the present moment to address the current consequences of that choice in your life. You still can radically accept who you are at this very moment while you do those things.

FORGIVENESS

Forgiveness is related to acceptance. When I needed a clearer sense of how forgiveness works, as I often do, I turned to my journal and asked Source:

Me: Source, can you talk to me about forgiveness? What is forgiveness?

Source: Forgiveness is the act of releasing the emotional burden you are carrying based on a perceived wrong that has been done to you. Sometimes, there is a notion that forgiving another person is an act of generosity towards that person because you are releasing them from the debt of the emotional wrong they did to you. In terms of the emotional debt of the other person, this type of forgiveness and its benefit only occurs when the other person is aware that they have been forgiven. If the act of forgiveness is never conveyed to the other person, then the other person cannot consciously receive the benefit of forgiveness. Please notice I used the word consciously. When a person consciously and genuinely forgives someone, there is an energetic change and benefit to the other person, even if they are not conscious or aware of the act of forgiveness. But this happens on the subconscious level, and the recipient of the forgiveness will not be consciously aware of the forgiveness unless they are told it has occurred.

Me: I think I understand. What I hear you saying is that there is always a benefit to the act of forgiveness, but the act of forgiveness is most powerful when it is done consciously, and all Beings involved are aware that forgiveness has occurred.

Source: Yes, the most powerful forgiveness is done in full presence, Being to Being. But I do want to bring up a key point. When most people think of forgiveness, it is the notion that they are releasing someone else from their emotional burden. This can be the case, but it can also be the case that the other person carries no emotional burden for the act you are forgiving. The act that was the emotional mountain for you may be a molehill, or even less, to them. The only emotional burden you can be sure of when it comes to forgiveness is the one that you are carrying yourself related to whatever needs to be forgiven.

What I am getting at is the *paradox of Forgiveness. By forgiving another Being, the burden released is the one you have been carrying.*

Me: Wow, I never thought of it that way before. I always thought that by not forgiving someone, somehow, I was holding an emotional chip over their head, so to speak. That my lack of forgiveness gave me a leg up on them. Somehow, I was superior when, in fact, it was just the opposite. I was doing most of the emotional damage to myself. That makes me question a lot of things, but are there some cases where you should just never forgive something?

Source: What do you think?

Me: Well, if I look at it your way now, by not forgiving, I am only emotionally hurting myself, but some things seem so horrible, so egregious, that they should never be forgiven. Like rape, or murder, or incest, or maybe some horrible violation of trust.

Source: The emotional burden you carry by not forgiving is your own. You can forgive something but still do everything in your power to ensure it never happens again, or the person that committed the act faces the full consequences of their actions. I also didn't say forgiveness is always easy, some of those acts you mention are terrible, but you will still carry the emotional burden, for the most part, by not forgiving.

Me: I guess I understand what you are saying, but there seems to me to be some things I could never forgive someone for. It seems there would be certain things that would be unforgivable.

Source: Yes, it would seem that way, and if you want to carry that emotional burden, then that is up to you. It is your experience to have. I am just answering your questions.

Me: That is a bit of a hard pill to swallow. I think it is going to take some time, but I do see the logic, and it feels right to me. I just don't know if I will be able to always do it.

Source: Then consider it a practice. The practice of forgiveness, and remember everything you forgive is a burden you are setting down.

Me: Okay, on paper, I understand all of this, and it makes sense, but from a practical standpoint, how do I deal with people who I vehemently disagree with or who have done something to hurt me, the people I care about, the environment, or the world?

Source: It goes back to your answer from just a few sentences ago. You must unconditionally accept every Being as they are in this very moment and know that the Being Equation means that they could be no other way in this present moment. However, you are also the Being that you are in the present moment as well, with your own set of values and life experiences. Although you unconditionally accept the other Being, it does not mean you condone or agree with or support them. Nor does it mean you don't wish they had done things differently. Although there is acceptance of the action, for every action, there is also a reaction. Your reaction will be based on the sum total of all the variables that make you the Being you are, your Life Events, your Egoic Interpretations, your Physical Body, your Inputs, your Environment, and your Spirit. Everything that makes you the Being that you are creates your reaction. You can accept your reaction in that moment because the Being Equation says it could be no other way.

Me: I think I have this. What you're saying is that you can accept another's action and forgive them, but not have to like or condone their action.

Source: Correct.

Me: You are also saying we can accept and forgive, but we also need to know and understand that there are consequences for every action.

Source: Yes. You can accept that your spouse had an affair. You can forgive your spouse for having an affair, but just because you have accepted and forgiven the action does not mean you need to stay married to your spouse. Every action has consequences.

You know, we have been talking about accepting and forgiving others, but we should also talk about forgiving oneself. Everything we are talking about also applies to forgiving yourself.

Me: That's true. Again, I had never thought of it this way.

Source: Most people don't. Most people have an easier time forgiving others and can't even accept and forgive themselves for the smallest transgressions. They beat themselves up for years and pile on the emotional burdens and are not even aware they do it. The Being Equation shows you that you are not the same person you were ten years ago, so why don't you forgive that old self? Why are you still carrying the emotional burden of a decision made years ago by a person you no longer are? What becomes even more treacherous is that you use the morals, values, and standards of your present self to judge the decisions and behavior of your past self, not taking into account that you are a very different person.

Me: That is true. My forty-five-year-old self cringes at some of the choices my twenty-five-year-old self made, but I am a very different person than I was at twenty-five. So, what should I do about that?

Source: Realize that and view your twenty-five-year-old self as exactly who it is, a different person. Allow the person you are now to forgive the person you were then, just as if you had forgiven a different person because you *are* forgiving a different person. Stop carrying the emotional burden and quit being so hard on yourself. I can assure you that the twenty-five-year-old you is not carrying an emotional burden because the twenty-five-year-old you does not even exist anymore.

Me: So, you are saying, just like we forgive others, we can forgive ourselves?

Source: That is exactly what I am saying. You are a different person from day to day, different Inputs, different Life Events. Look how much someone can change in a year. If you're striving for personal and Spiritual growth and doing it right, the person you are now has grown over the past few years. Don't hold the person you were to the standards of the person you are now. Every decision is made in the context of who you are at a particular moment in time.

Me: Right, and this starts getting back to acceptance in the Being Equation.

Source: Yes.

Me: Every decision that any Being makes is the result of the sum total of all the variables in the Being Equation for that Being up to that very moment in time. All the Inputs, Life Events, and Egoic Interpretations lead to the Being's actions in that moment, and given the exact same conditions, any Being would have made that same choice. Therefore, if we can accept the decision, we can forgive the decision, and we have to accept because the Being Equation shows it could be no other way. If it could be no other way, then we should forgive because we are carrying around the emotional burden for no reason.

Source: Exactly. You have been paying attention.

The truth related in the conversation above regarding accepting and forgiving yourself has been one of the most impactful aspects of the Being Equation in my life. When I was seventeen years old, I had to make a decision that created the greatest single regret of my life. As a result of that decision and the actions that followed, I did not see or speak to my sister, brother, or stepmother for twenty-two years.

Out of respect for them and their privacy, I will share no other specific details around the events, other than to say what transpired was no fault of theirs. It was all on me.

After I made it, I felt ashamed of my decision. I felt ashamed that I had let my father down, who had passed away from cancer months before I made this decision. I felt ashamed because I was not there to be a big brother, a protector to my little sister and brother as they grew up without a father. I felt ashamed because I had betrayed the love and trust of my stepmother and her extended family, who had embraced me over the previous twelve years.

I carried this guilt and shame with me for twenty-two years. As I think about it now, that decision and the shame and regret around it made me not like the person I was. I could not forgive myself or accept myself, and therefore, I did not feel worthy of acceptance by others. I realize now how this kept me from fully showing up in the world because I was afraid that if I did, someone would see right through me and see this terrible decision I had made.

After twenty-two years, the pain and regret of not seeing my sister, brother, and stepmother and not being in their lives, coupled with some inner personal work, led me to send a letter to my stepmother. Her love, acceptance, and forgiveness of me was a beautiful example of the power love, acceptance, and forgiveness can have on a life, my life. Her love, acceptance, and forgiveness were crucial in allowing me to love, accept, and forgive myself.

This deeply personal example also taught me something else. You cannot have a discussion about love, acceptance, and forgiveness without addressing shame. I realized this when I was thinking and writing about this experience and saw how many times I used the word "ashamed." It made me see that shame is often what keeps us from beginning the process of acceptance and forgiveness. Shame was what held me back from beginning the process of reconnecting with my stepmother, brother, and sister. Shame held me back from sending that letter for twenty-two years.

SHAME

Dr. Brené Brown is arguably the most well-known shame researcher on the planet, and she defines shame as "the intensely painful feeling or experience of believing that we are flawed and therefore unworthy of love and belonging." Simply reading this definition makes my heart feel heavy.

Often, shame is what blocks us from even moving into and exploring the past Life Events and our Egoic Interpretation around those events because we don't want to relive the feeling of shame they create in us. By not doing this, by not moving into the shame, we are perpetuating those feelings of being unworthy of love and belonging, and therefore, not allowing ourselves to move into the phases of acceptance and forgiveness.

Please don't get me wrong. Shame does not always come before acceptance and forgiveness. In fact, there are plenty of times that things happen that we need to accept and forgive within ourselves that do not generate shame, but when it is present, it has to be acknowledged and addressed. One of my mentors, Philip McKernan, says that, to address shame, you have to shine a light on it and bring it out into the open. When things that cause shame are shared with others, the shame loses its power. I agree with him. For me, this process starts with admitting to yourself that you have shame around a Life Event. It is only after you admit it to yourself that you can share it with others.

The other tough thing about shame is that we can have shame that originates from things that are done to us through no fault of our own or from the poor behavior of others that reflect poorly on us. Whatever the cause of shame, the first step has to be acknowledging that the shame exists. It is only through this acknowledgment that you can start the process of moving into acceptance and forgiveness.

Shame is a big topic, and my purpose here is to make you aware of the role shame can play in the process of love, acceptance, and forgiveness. Having this awareness is a good place to start when exploring your relationship with shame. If you would like to explore it further, I encourage you to start with the extensive work of Dr. Brené Brown.

LOVE

LOVE
Why do we rush?
Where are we going?
What do we have to do?
What more do we need than the land,
a bit of sun,
a few logs to warm our hearth,
some bread to break with friends,
a cup of wine, a pint of beer,
oh, and love, we must have love or our hearts wither.
Love of family,
Love of friends,
Love of nature,
Love of life,
Love of ourselves.
Love.

I know, it probably seems odd to you as the reader to have a poem show up in this book.

I don't write poems on a regular basis, maybe a handful of times a year, but when poems do come to me, they are often in a flurry of inspiration and emotion. Some place or event has triggered something within me that wants to come out as a poem, and this one is no different—but why a poem?

I believe words are incredibly powerful, but they can also be incredibly clunky. To me, a poem is an attempt to distill a feeling, emotion, or idea into a very concentrated essence, kind of like vanilla extract is the distilled essence of the vanilla bean. All of the sunshine and nutrients and energy that the orchids of the species Vanilla use to produce a flower that, when pollinated, eventually produces a seed pod that is harvested and dried. The pod is then ground, and the essential oils are extracted to produce the powerful and flavorful vanilla extract.

For me, poems are the extract, the essence, of an experience. I am typically in a new place or have had an experience that calls to be distilled and extracted in a way that can't be done with long-form writing. It is something I want to remember and share, to recreate the feeling and context of all that is happening within and around me. The result is a poem.

I wrote the poem above in Ireland on June 22, 2019. I had arrived in Ireland the day before and was working to overcome jet lag. I awoke at three o'clock in the morning and started to walk around the city of Dublin around five o'clock. I aimlessly wandered the streets for about two hours before stopping at the Stage Door Cafe for a full Irish breakfast. The streets were empty except for the occasional heroin addicts setting up their tents or finding a bench to sleep on after a long night. I distinctly remember seeing a man and a woman setting up their tent on the sidewalk, no different than if they were out in the wilderness backpacking, except they moved slowly and deliberately, as if they were in a great fog.

After finishing my breakfast, I wandered the grounds of Trinity College and happened upon the Great Library housing the *Book of Kells*. By luck, I arrived just as the doors were opening, so I had the place mostly to myself. As a lover of words, I was amazed to see a book before me that had been handwritten around 800 AD, which I was viewing inside a case 1,200 years later.

I left the exhibit and continued to stroll Trinity College. I found a small courtyard with a lovely tree and bench, so I sat down there. As I was sitting on the bench and reflecting on my experiences over the prior forty-eight hours, the poem above emerged. I didn't intend to write about love. The scenes of the morning made me realize how short and impermanent our individual lives are. I wondered what I really needed in my life to make my one, short life feel worthwhile and content. Sitting there on that bench, I went from thinking about how busy and crazy we make our lives (to get all the material things we think we want and need) to realizing how few material things we actually need, to ultimately realizing the thing we want and need most is not a material thing at all. It is love.

It sounds cheesy to say, but it really does all begin and end with love. Love is what allows us to start moving through shame, acceptance, and forgiveness. Love is what grows within us as we start to forgive and accept ourselves and others.

Through love, acceptance, and forgiveness of yourself and others, you bring more positive energy and power into your life. More energy you can focus toward growing and improving all aspects of your life. More energy you can bring into your life to love yourself and those around you. Love.

CHAPTER 10

FEELINGS AND EMOTIONS

How are feelings and emotions related to the Being Equation? When I had questions myself, I turned to my journal and asked Source:

Source: Every Being is a combination of a Physical Body and a Spiritual Body. There are stimuli that only your Spiritual Body perceives. The Spiritual Body is not only connected to this physical world, it is also connected to the Spiritual world, which is much larger and infinite on a scale that your Physical Body cannot comprehend. Your Spiritual Body receives stimuli both from the Spiritual Bodies of other Beings in this world and the greater infinite Spiritual world you are not aware of but connected to. You are connected to Source Energy, and your Spiritual Body receives stimuli from this place as well. These stimuli from Source Energy are internal stimuli because they are not originating from another Spiritual Being but a connection to Source. External Spiritual signals come from other Spiritual Beings you interact with in the physical form you have now.

Me: So, our Spiritual Body uses a whole different set of senses than our Physical Body, but we receive information just the same?

Source: Yes.

Me: So then where does that feeling of knowing come from, or maybe how can we get better at feeling the Spiritual stuff?

Source: The feeling of knowing comes from your direct connection to Source. Think of it this way. Your Physical Body sends you signals all the time, and you have to decide whether to listen to them. For example, your body sends you a signal when you should stop eating or what you should eat based on how you feel, then you decide if you will listen to that signal. Many of you rarely listen to it, but that is a choice. Your Spiritual body does the same thing. The feelings you have are signals, like being full, but it is up to you whether you listen to them.

The Spiritual signals are happening all the time, like your physical signals. All you have to do to get more of the signals is to pay more attention. To carry on the food analogy, sometimes people go to diet and fitness centers to reset their physical selves. The decisions on what and how much to eat are taken care of, and it works as a removal of distraction.

The same is true for the Spiritual Body. Meditation retreats or other practices that focus on removing distractions and paying attention to the Spiritual Body are like fitness camps as well. All the outside distractions are removed, and focus on the Spiritual Body can be applied. You can do this alone, just as you can diet alone. It takes more willpower, however. If you want to get good at it, do the same things you would do to help your Physical Body. Remove the junk food from the house. Have healthy snacks in the fridge. Plan your meals in advance and get into a routine. For your Spiritual Body, remove the distraction of technology, have books, music, or other materials on hand for reading about and connecting with Spirit, and have journal questions and prompts ready. Set up a Spiritual space in your home that you can use for whatever Spiritual practice you choose. Plan time in your schedule for your Spiritual Body. Your Spiritual Body needs attention and nourishment, just like your Physical Body. As you become more in tune with your Spiritual Body, you will become more aware of the cues your Spiritual Body is providing. It then becomes your choice of how to respond to them.

CHANGING OUR EMOTIONS

Me: I see that feelings can arise from both our Physical Body and our Spiritual Body, but what about emotions? What are they, and where do they come from?

Source: Emotions are the representation of the current state of our conscious mind. This current state creates a physical manifestation of sensations in your body. Since your Physical Body is a sensory mechanism, you "feel" this sensory expression, and this creates "feelings." Feelings are the physical manifestation of emotions.

Want to change how you feel? Change the emotion, and your feelings will change. You cannot control your emotions at the moment they arise. Emotions that arise in the present are the result of all the past stories or Egoic Interpretations you have from your past Life Events. Again, you do not control the emotion that arises in the present. You can influence what emotion may arise by changing your Egoic Interpretation of Life Events, or you can control your physical reaction to the emotion, but you cannot control the emotion.

* * *

In the dialogue above, Source brings up a critical point. You cannot control your emotions at the moment they arise. You may be able to suppress them quickly, but you do not control them at that moment.

Let's look at a famous example to clarify this point. In the 1890s, the Russian physiologist, Ivan Pavlov, performed a series of experiments involving dogs, food, stimuli, and saliva. What he discovered came to be coined "classical conditioning." Pavlov discovered that he could use non-related stimuli to signal to the dog that it was going to be fed. He would ring a bell before he was going to feed a dog, and the dog would begin to salivate exactly as if the bowl of food were placed before it. The dog would have the emotional response of excitement and anticipation to the bell, resulting in the physical response of increased salivation and other preparatory physical reactions for eating. This response could also be de-conditioned, meaning that even if the dog had learned to associate the bell with food, if the bell was rung and no food appeared and this continued to happen, eventually, the dog would no longer salivate. The emotion to the bell is no longer excitement and anticipation, and therefore, the physical response is not triggered.

This is exactly what happens to us as Beings all the time. We receive a stimulus, and that stimulus is compared against all of the knowledge and past experience we have in our subconscious mind. There is a lot of information in the subconscious, so to save time, our subconscious defaults to the program or the Egoic Interpretation we have built around that stimulus over time and feeds that Story to our conscious mind. Our conscious mind generates the appropriate feeling and begins the physical/mental response to that feeling.

So, how do we change our feelings?

1. Change the Egoic Interpretation (Story) around a given stimulus.
2. Gain awareness and control over our physical response.

The first option involves changing the Story or Egoic Interpretation in advance or before the stimulus occurs, and the second option involves having the awareness to pause and not immediately react to the emotion. *The paradox is, that in the exact present moment, we cannot control the emotion that arises.* We either have to change the Story before the stimulus arrives, or we have to use awareness to change the feeling afterward. There is a toll and a potential danger to controlling our feelings, which we will discuss further.

THE PARABLE OF BOB: OPTION ONE

Let's look at an example to clarify how we can use the two options above to change our feelings. Imagine you have a supervisor at work named Bob. Bob is always in a sour mood. He never has anything good to say about anyone or anything. You have never seen Bob smile, and he is always critical of the work that anyone in the office turns in to him. When you first started working for Bob, you did everything possible to impress him. You went far above and beyond what was expected on every report you turned in to him, and he always found something in your work to criticize. After six months or so, you stopped trying to impress Bob, and you became resigned to the fact that he was a jerk. Other people in the office had tried to tell you he was a jerk and that it wasn't you, but you thought you could win him over. Instead, Bob crushed you.

Now, whenever you see Bob or even think of Bob when you are not at the office, you feel angry. You can feel your blood pressure rise, you start to clench your jaw, and your face flushes red. Before you know it, the simple thought of Bob puts you in an angry, bad mood. In this example, either the physical presence or the thought of Bob is your stimulus. It stimulates the emotion of anger followed by the physical manifestations or "feelings" of anger, including elevated blood pressure, clenched jaw, and a flushed face. You then become angry yourself and in a bad mood as a result. How could we use option one, change our Egoic Interpretation, to improve the situation around Bob?

Now imagine that you are at a family dinner and you start talking to your Uncle Phil. Uncle Phil asks you how work is going, and you let him know you switched jobs about a year ago and now you work at XYZ Corporation. Uncle Phil says that in high school, thirty years ago, he was friends with a guy named Bob that works at XYZ Corporation and asks if you happen to know him. Oh boy, do you ever know him. You tell Uncle Phil about how Bob has treated you this past year. How you did everything in your power to impress Bob, and how Bob is always negative, and how no one at XYZ Corporation likes Bob. In fact, just the thought of Bob makes you angry right now at this family dinner. Uncle Phil says he is sorry to hear that working with Bob is a challenge and then he asks you the following question: do you know what happened to Bob twenty years ago? You realize that you don't know *anything* about Bob outside of work. No one at XYZ Corporation does. Then, your Uncle Phil lays the following story on you:

Twenty years ago, Bob had been happily married to his high school sweetheart, Betty. They had two children, a boy and a girl. At that time, Bob was working at a different company and was doing quite well. Everyone there liked him and requested to be on his work team. Everything seemed perfect in Bob's world, or at least he thought so.

Bob came home from work one day to find Betty and the kids were gone. All that she left was a note saying that she had found someone else. She moved across the country with the two children and filed for divorce. Bob fought in court to get custody of the children, but Betty told some lies about how he treated the children, and he was banned from visitation with the children. He hadn't seen or heard from them in twenty years. After the experience, Bob began to withdraw from the outside world, just as anyone would. His performance at his previous job suffered, and after a few years, he got fired. The only place that would hire him was XYZ Corporation, at a lower job title and with much less pay. Bob had been beaten down by life and the lies of others.

After Uncle Phil's story, you now have some real sympathy for Bob. What an ordeal to live through. No wonder he is always bitter and angry. Knowing all of this, Bob's behavior makes more sense, and you actually have some sympathy for him. Now when you see him, you don't feel angry, you feel sad. You realize it's not you that Bob doesn't like. He doesn't like life, and that is a sad place to be.

In this scenario, all that changed was your Story about Bob. However, that change in Story now changes the emotion you feel from the stimulus of Bob walking in the room. The emotion is sympathy, and the feeling is sadness. You understand that Bob was not always like this, and some very tough things happened in his life to turn him into the person he is now.

THE PARABLE OF BOB: OPTION TWO

Let's look at an example using option two, gaining awareness and control over our physical response. In this scenario, you know that you get angry every time you see or think about Bob. As you feel that initial emotion of anger, you close your eyes and take a few deep breaths. You consciously acknowledge the emotion of anger and then consciously calm yourself through breathing and mindfulness. You offer some internal words of kindness to Bob, or you focus your attention on something that brings you gratitude and joy. You are able to keep the initial emotion of anger from turning into the physical manifestation of anger and keep your calm and composure. This is absolutely possible with awareness and practice, but realize that this takes mental and physical energy to accomplish, which brings us to the potential pitfall from using option two.

Option two requires one to be constantly aware of one's emotions as they arise and then use techniques to control those emotions before they turn into feelings. There are definitely situations in which controlling our feelings is beneficial, but it is also important to understand the energetic costs, both short- and long-term of trying to control our feelings. In some cases, controlling our feelings is beneficial, for example, when responding to an email or conversation that makes us initially angry. It is often important to take some time and respond when the initial wave of emotion and feeling has passed in order not to say or do something out of strong feeling that we would regret later. I have also gone to the other extreme when dealing with a very positive emotion, being conscious not to allow myself to feel too happy or too excited about something to try and minimize the disappointment or sadness once the event is over. I have actually limited my feelings of happiness and joy so that the fall from my peak high of happiness would not be as far to the trough of letdown once the event was over. It sounds like a silly thing to do, but maybe you have done it yourself.

If I am being honest, this is something I did for many years. My wife and friends used to describe me as very even-keeled and steady. I never got too upset or angry about the negative things, but I also never got super excited or joyful about the positive things. I was Mr. Steady. I didn't realize it at the time, but this was a defense mechanism I had built over many years. As for all of us, there were some tough, emotional times in my childhood and young adult life. Now, I realize I did not know how to deal with the emotions and feelings I was having. I felt alone, and the feelings of anger, grief, and sadness were painful. I realize now that I essentially numbed my feelings by limiting the response I would have to emotions. I walled off and protected part of myself so that it would not have to deal with painful emotions and feelings. However, by walling that part of myself off, it also meant that I did not fully experience the positive emotions and feelings. I was not showing up to experience my life fully, to feel my life fully, to enjoy my life fully. It took serious self-reflection and the help of a great mentor for me to see this. It was not something I was even aware of, but I am now.

I have alluded to the dangers of controlling your feelings; I want to be very clear, and I say this from my own personal experience and based on many conversations with others. Controlling your feelings, whether consciously or subconsciously, takes a tremendous amount of physical and emotional energy. If you suppress negative feelings, they will show up in your body and affect how you show up in the world.

I struggled with this issue for so many years. I lived a life that I thought I was supposed to live instead of the one I wanted to live, and the scary thing was that I was not even consciously aware of it. My mind and my body were giving me all the signs that I was not living in alignment with who I was, but I didn't know how to pay attention to the signs. I thought I was doing everything right, and by societal terms, I was. I had earned two advanced degrees, had a well-paying profession, had plenty of friends, and went to all the "right" social functions. I was married to a beautiful woman who had a great career as well.

THE SIGNS I MISSED

So, what were the signs that I was missing, or in hindsight, choosing to ignore?

I would wake up each morning not excited for the day ahead. There were many days where my mood would be very dark, what I would call depressed. Did this depression keep me from going to work and showing up for the people that needed me? In most cases, no, but I was definitely not showing up fully for those around me. I had, however, become a master at putting on a happy face and faking it, which was taking a heavy toll.

The physical symptoms were there as well. I had always been able to eat any foods I had wanted without ever suffering heartburn or indigestion. However, over the course of a year or so, I developed severe heartburn and acid reflux. Previously, I had been able to eat spicy foods and loved tomatoes and pizza and pasta, but all of that was now off the table. Even the sight of them would give me heartburn. I had enjoyed a morning coffee, but now a sip of coffee required a handful of antacids as a chaser to ease the heartburn. I went to see a gastroenterologist and had an endoscopy. I was diagnosed with gastroesophageal reflux disease (GERD), put on prescription medication with TUMS and Rolaids as needed, and had to change my diet.

During this same time, I had also been experiencing occasional chest pains even though I was in good shape physically. I could easily ride my bike thirty miles or go out for a five-mile run, but then I would be home and have chest pains. A stress test including an echocardiogram confirmed my heart was in great shape and no blockages. Now I realize that I was holding a tremendous amount of mental and emotional stress within my body, and it was causing these issues.

Through my upbringing, I learned to be a people pleaser and a very empathetic one at that. I also really enjoyed meeting people, and while this empathetic, people-pleasing background was great for building the relationships that being a real estate broker required, it also meant I internalized a lot of stress created by variables outside of my control.

Real estate transactions are complex and not only involve the wants and desires of your clients but also involve other agents, lenders, title companies, and the party on the opposite side of the transaction. There are often competing interests, and it becomes impossible to make everyone happy all the time. Although I intellectually knew this, I still tried to make everyone happy. I always felt responsible, even for things far outside my control. I internalized all of this stress and emotion and was available to my clients and everyone else 24/7. The result was the physical symptoms and damage I was inflicting on my body and Spirit. I was physically experiencing gastroesophageal reflux disease, chest pains, and mentally I felt depressed. I believe the depression was a symptom of my Spirit screaming at me that this was not the way it was meant to be.

I turned to alcohol far too many nights to try and numb my brain and feelings. Why do I tell you all of this? Because I want you to see that I didn't know any better. I thought that was just the way life was. That there is stress in every job. Life has its ups and downs. You are not going to wake up happy and excited every day. Sometimes we must do things we don't want to do.

The truth is, that's all bullshit. Life does not have to be stressful and a struggle. What you do for a living should not take a physical and emotional toll on you. Your job and your life should not give you acid reflux and chest pains. *That is not normal.*

You should be excited to get out of bed each morning. You should have a glass of wine because you enjoy it, not to numb your emotions from feeling stress and pain.

If I were reading this five years ago, here is where I would have said, "Easy for you to say, Sunshine. You have no idea everything I have to manage in my life." You may be thinking the same thing. True, I don't know, but it is your life, and the vast majority of things you have to manage are things you have chosen and are in your control.

I am not saying it will be easy or fast to change. It took you twenty, thirty, forty years to get to this point. You can't expect to unwind it overnight, but what is the alternative? Status quo. Poor mental and/or physical health, no excitement about a new day dawning?

But you can unwind it, it can all change, and it doesn't have to all be done tomorrow, but it can *start* tomorrow.

CHAPTER 11

ENERGY

I like to think of our emotional energy as a flowing stream. Every emotion that we are working to control in some way takes a diversion of water out of the stream. The size of the emotion we are trying to control is directly proportional to the amount of water diverted out of our emotional stream. If we have emotions that we have been suppressing for years or decades, then those emotions are still diverting water out of our emotional energy stream each and every day. This stream represents all of the emotional energy you can bring to your life each day, and the more diversions you have, the less emotional energy that is available for you to live each day.

A few years ago, my emotional stream was down to a small trickle. I had so many old diversions that I wasn't even aware of, and they were taking so much emotional energy to maintain each day, that I didn't have much emotional energy to give to my friends and family in the present. I was also a people pleaser and would suppress my own wants and desires to make those around me happy. This also takes a tremendous amount of emotional energy. What was left was a dull, emotional version of the person I really am. My emotional energy stream was running dry.

But here is the good news. The journey to understanding who you are is also the journey that will start removing those stream diversions. Once you start taking those diversions down, then all that emotional energy returns to your life, and you start having more and more emotional energy to bring to your life each day. Your stream can go from a trickle to a torrent. That is what has happened for me.

It is not all sunshine and rainbows. If you want to let your emotional stream flow, you have to be willing to experience the sorrow and sadness just as much as the joy and happiness. I am now, and life feels very different when you are fully here.

ENERGY DIVERSIONS

Energy diversions are caused by anything that you do not feel like you dealt with properly at the moment it occurred. If you think back on a Life Event and think there is something you wish you would have said or done differently, then there is an energy diversion there. These can be the smallest of interactions to the biggest events in your life. It could be anything from wishing you would have given the homeless woman with her dog a dollar when you saw them sitting on the sidewalk at Christmas last year, to wishing you would have held your father's hand and told him how much you loved him and how much he meant to you before he passed away. Everything left undone, unsaid, said wrong, or done wrong no matter how large or how small, creates an energy diversion in the present moment. We are not always, rarely in fact, aware that these diversions are occurring, but they are. You may have consciously forgotten about them, but your subconscious has not.

How does not giving a dollar to a homeless woman and her dog create an energy diversion? You might be reading something or hear someone mention the word generosity, and that little voice in your head blurts out, *You're not generous, you couldn't even give that poor homeless woman and her dog a dollar at Christmas. What kind of person are you?* And it keeps happening over and over. One split-second choice about a dollar, and you are "not generous."

Start to pay attention, and you will find what seems like trivial events all through your life, things that you wish you would have done differently pop back up in the present moment and take your focus away, and make you feel bad. Well, how does this take energy? Anything that takes your focus out of the present moment is taking your energy. All you have is your focus. Where your focus goes, your energy flows. Whatever pulls your focus out of this present moment is taking your energy. Things you wish you would have done differently are a huge source of diversion of your energy.

This is so important because, as physical Beings, the amount of energy you have is finite. To put it in simple terms, you only have so much energy to allocate each day. This is because you are a Spiritual Being in physical form. The physical form takes energy that is different from Spiritual energy. Even the most enlightened Spiritual Beings that have taken physical form leave the physical form eventually.

ENERGY, SPIRIT, AND THE PHYSICAL BODY

To understand this relationship between energy, Spirit, and the

Physical Body, I had a discussion with Source and the dialogue is below.

Me: Can you talk about the interplay between physical and Spiritual Energy?

Source: This could get complicated, but let's try to keep it as simple as possible. As we discussed before, you have both a Physical and a Spiritual Body. Both your Physical and your Spiritual Bodies require energy, just as all things do. Everything is ultimately made of energy. For you to be in this physical world, your Spiritual Body is intertwined with your Physical Body. Each of these two bodies, the Spiritual and Physical, require their own type of care and nourishment, but because they are so intertwined, there is also tremendous overlap between the two, meaning certain things you do to nourish the Physical affect the Spiritual and vice versa. This also means the state of health of one, so to speak, greatly affects the other. You can often see this interaction in the way that someone carries themself physically. If the Spirit is feeling sad, depressed, and beaten down by life, then the body will be stooped, shoulders slumped, beaten down. If you can change the Spirit, then the physical form immediately, almost instantaneously, follows.

The Spiritual Body is far stronger than the Physical Body, and the amount of energy it can contain is beyond imagination. Just look at Mother Theresa or Gandhi—physically meek, Spiritually mighty.

Me: I see what you mean, but I feel like we have gotten a bit off track on energy.

Source: Well, it is not a small topic. Everything is energy. An energy diversion is like a muscle knot in the Physical Body. You have to massage it out, or it will keep hurting and taking energy. Here's how. When something comes into your consciousness that you don't feel good about, don't run from it or block it. Instead, focus on it. Address it, and if you can't address it right then, write it down and make a plan. Journal about it and do something concrete. You didn't give the homeless woman and her dog a dollar, so resolve to give a dollar to every homeless person you see now or plan to volunteer at the homeless shelter. You didn't have the conversation with your father? Close your eyes and call him into your heart and have it now. You feel bad about some mean things you said to your sister twenty years ago? Call her now or write a letter to her and apologize. This is how you deal with these energy diversions—head on. And continue to be very curious about the diversions you don't consciously know you have; seek those out and deal with them, too. The more energy diversions you remove, the more energy you have for your everyday life, and the more present and focused you can be.

The other way to deal with them is to keep from creating them in the first place. As you become more connected to your Spirit and intuition, you will know what to do in the present moment—then, it is a matter of listening and doing it.

* * *

The reality is that no matter how hard we try, each of us will make decisions in the moment that we would like to change. Don't beat yourself up about it. Just take steps to fix it. It is all we can do, and sometimes the lessons we learn from our mistakes and how we fix them are the most valuable lessons of all.

Exercise: Take a moment to identify an energy diversion in your life. An easy way to find one is to think about a Life Event that, each time it happens, it makes you say, "I really should _____."

For example, my high school basketball coach, Coach French, was an extremely important mentor in my life. He believed in me and supported me through a difficult time. I realize that I have never told him how important and meaningful he was to me during that period, and now it has been almost thirty years. Every time I think of him, I say to myself, *I really should send him a letter or give him a call and tell him how much that time meant to me.* Then, I beat myself up each time I don't do it. That, my friends, is an energy diversion that is at least twenty-five years old and one that can be fixed easily.

To take this one step further, the next question is to get curious as to why you haven't done it. For me, there is guilt and shame that I have not reached out to this person in twenty-five years. I am embarrassed. Can you see how a little curiosity to go just a little deeper can really get to the core of an issue?

So, what is the energy diversion that you are going to address right now?

CHAPTER 12

RELATIONSHIPS

You have a relationship with every object and/or Being in your environment, whether you are conscious of it or not. Most of us are not fully conscious of the relationships we have with different things or Beings in our environment.

The keys to great relationships are to:

1. Consciously examine the relationship you have with each Being or thing in your environment.
2. Determine if the relationship is positive and serving you or negative and detrimental to you.
3. Take the steps necessary to improve the relationship or end the relationship.

It is a common saying that relationships are complicated. Actually, relationships are simple. What is complicated is dealing with the emotional complexities that arise in a relationship, but everyone knows on a very basic level, whether a relationship is positive or negative. Where things get "complicated" is how to take the necessary actions to enhance or end a relationship and how to deal with the emotions this creates.

Although it is not always easy, this is the work that will change your life. Whether anyone wants to admit it or not, those Beings we spend the most time with have the greatest impact on our lives. They can either raise us up or drag us down. The good news is that we choose who to surround ourselves with. It's a choice each of us is empowered to make. We just have to do it. The same can be said of the things in our life. We choose the objects that occupy our environment. We can choose whether a thing stays or goes.

THE OBJECTS IN OUR ENVIRONMENT

If it is not a living being, it falls into the "object" category. Once we view the world this way and realize that *every single object* in our environment has an energetic and emotional effect on us, then we can see that changing the objects in the environment can change who we are.

This sounds a bit crazy. How can changing a few objects in our environment change who we are? If you are sitting in your home right now, take a moment to look around. As you look at each object or group of objects, check in with your body and see if the objects bring up an emotional charge when you focus on them. Is there a Story that comes into your mind when you see a certain object? For example, as I write this, there is a picture of my wife and two of her friends on the windowsill. One of her friends is holding her baby daughter. They are all sitting on the grass and looking at the camera and smiling. The friend holding her baby daughter passed away about a month after this photo was taken. She was in her late thirties. Every time I see this photo, it reminds me how precious and short life can be. I also see a jumbled stack of books, journals, boxes, and papers that has been piled on the counter beside the refrigerator for months. This cluster of objects is a reminder that I still have not sorted through all of these things and strums the strings of the procrastination story that plays in my mind.

If you doubt that an object can have power over how you feel, look at the success of Marie Kondo and her books, most notably, *The Life-Changing Magic of Tidying Up: The Japanese Art of Decluttering and Organizing*. Her book series has sold over four million copies around the world, and she was named as one of *Time Magazine's* one hundred Most Influential People in the world in 2015. All these people are not drawn to her work because it is a simple, quick hit list of the top ten things you need to do to get your house clean and organized. People resonate with it because, in Kondo's own words, "the question of what you want to own is actually the question of how you want to live your life." The philosophy that Kondo teaches is quite simple. Focus your attention on each object in your environment by picking it up or physically touching it. Be mindful of the emotions and feelings that the object sparks within you. Keep only those objects that speak to the heart, and discard those items that no longer spark joy. Thank them for their service, then let them go.

Why has Kondo's method gained so much popularity and attention? Because it can immediately change how you feel in your environment. Most Beings are not aware that they have a relationship with every object in their environment and that every object, every single thing, in their environment sparks an emotion within them.

Still not convinced about having a relationship with things? Try it again. Look around your environment again. Pick an object and see what Story comes to mind. I see our coffee mug collection. One is a brightly colored terrazzo pottery mug with blues, reds, and greens we picked up in Mexico on vacation. Each time my wife uses it, she literally says that the mug makes her happy because she thinks of Mexico. There is also a turquoise pottery mug that my wife made in pottery class. Another brown pottery mug with a tree etched on it that we bought in her hometown in Pennsylvania, another oddly shaped pottery mug that would normally be in the discard pile, but it was the first mug I made myself. All of these mugs spark a unique emotion for me.

What about your closet? Do you have clothes in there that spark feelings within you? I have a suit I bought twenty-three years ago that no longer fits me. I keep it because my uncle, who passed away a few years ago, helped me pick out the suit and matching tie. Each time I see it, it reminds me of him, but it also reminds me I am about twenty pounds heavier than I used to be.

Every object in our environment contributes to our environment. You have a relationship with each one. Everything you see and touch has a Story and energy associated with it, and these objects are conscious reminders to us of those stories and feelings. Why does it feel so good to declutter and purge certain objects from our environment? Because you are literally removing the objects that are emotionally and energetically weighing you down. You feel lighter and refreshed because you are emotionally and energetically lighter, allowing you to bring more energy and to be more present in your world.

THE BEINGS IN OUR ENVIRONMENT

By now, I hope you realize that every Being in your environment has an effect on the Being that you are. Our relationships with other Beings in our lives can be one of the most difficult things to navigate. Family relationships, marriages, divorces, parents, bosses, teachers, children, and coworkers—all of these different categories—set up expectations created by society and our own pre-existing beliefs. It can be mentally and physically overwhelming to think about how we need to show up differently in the world for each of the relationships that we have in this world, so I am going to propose something which may seem controversial.

Don't think about it. *Don't think about how you are supposed to show up for each of these relationships in terms of societal or familial expectations.* Don't think about the roles and responsibilities that each of these societal labels produces. In reality, these different societal and familial roles and associated expectations actually create a competing set of demands within themselves. Think about it: isn't the time, dedication, and energy required to make you the ideal employee and coworker at work competing with the same time, dedication, and energy required to make you the ideal parent or partner at home?

What no one wants to admit to themselves, and our society certainly doesn't support, is the truth that there is not enough time to be all things to all people. *So, the answer is to stop trying to do it all. Be who you are to yourself.* We only have so much energy to dedicate to our relationships with others. It is critically important that we become highly aware of how we are dedicating our energy to other Beings, and just like the objects in our environment, how each of the Beings in our environment is making us feel. Do they spark joy within us, and if not, what can we do to change that feeling, or do we need to let them go?

Initially, this may be jarring for some of you to hear, as it tends to contradict the lessons that many of us learned growing up. As a result of being a people pleaser, I expended nearly all of my emotional energy trying to satisfy others, and my emotional energy tank ran dry. The result was that the Beings in my life that I truly cared about were the recipients of the little emotional energy I had left in the tank. I was not making any conscious decisions about how my emotional energy was being spent and who was the recipient of that energy. Most of us live our lives exactly like this. The good news is that the solution to this problem is very simple, and it comes back to the central question of this book: *who am I?* As you gain clarity on who you are, and you also realize, as the Being Equation shows, that the Beings in your life are part of making you who you are in this present moment, then you can start consciously choosing the Beings and relationships that make you who you want to be.

I would like to make you abundantly aware of something in case you are not aware of it already, and I would like you to spend a few minutes really letting this settle and land deep within you. Are you ready? *You cannot be all things to all people.* You only have so much energy to give, so you have to make some choices.

You cannot do and be everything all the time. I do not mean for this to sound glib, but most of us do not want to face this reality. We are told we can and need to do it all. We are told in high school and college that we need to be in every club, take every class, play every sport, be a leader, be in the musical, and the play so we can get into a good school or get a great job. We are then told we need to put in the extra time at work, make it to every soccer game, have romantic dates, make it home for the holidays, go on the work trips, make it to the office Christmas Party, bake something for the bake sale, take the kids to basketball practice, sew the costume for the school play, work out, have perfect skin, and play poker and smoke cigars with the guys, and this is all normal and expected. This is impossible, and if I am the first to tell you this, shame on the world. You cannot do everything, and if you felt like you have done a pretty good job of it to this point, you are fooling yourself. Maybe a shadow of you has done these things, but all of you has not. There is no way the full, energetic Being that you are has been able to show up and be fully present for all of these activities. It was only a shadow of you, and the world deserves more than a shadow. So, what is the solution? Awareness and choices.

1. Be keenly aware that every interaction with another Being takes energy.
2. Decide who you want to be in the world and who deserves your energy.
3. Do those things that support you in who you are.
4. Be fully present in all that you do.

Since we have been discussing emotional energy and the importance of deciding how to spend it, this is a great time to reveal another paradox to you. By realizing that you are the most important person in your world and by taking care of your emotional needs first, you will have more energy to give to the relationships that matter to you most.

THE AIRPLANE ANALOGY

If you have flown in the last twenty years, then you have heard the flight attendant say in the safety briefing that, "In the event of a cabin depressurization, an oxygen mask will fall from the panel above your head. Please secure your own mask before securing the masks of those around you." This is sage advice.

Consider the airplane analogy. If you don't put on your own oxygen mask and instead pass out, how much good will you be to those around you? Whereas, if you get your mask on first, then you will be able to assist those around you with their masks, ensuring their well-being and safety. If you are emotionally drained and in a low state yourself, how much emotional energy and support do you have to lend to a significant other, friend, or child in need? Wouldn't you have much more to offer if your emotional batteries were fully charged?

The key is to have the awareness to realize when you need to get your own oxygen mask on. Most of us see that oxygen mask fall from the overhead compartment and blissfully ignore it because we don't have time for an oxygen mask even though it is the *only* thing we desperately need at the moment.

What does putting on your own oxygen mask look like? It means realizing that doing things that recharge your own emotional batteries is not optional; it is *required*. It means that an hour for a yoga class is not selfish because you have more emotional energy for your children after the class than before. It means that an afternoon spent fishing or reading by yourself is not selfish but necessary for you to recharge your emotional energy. It means realizing that not taking the time you need for yourself and not showing up fully in the world is much more selfish than taking the time you need because you are depriving those you are in relationships with of the full presence of you. *You are actually more selfish when you don't take time for yourself because you like the thought of doing it all more than the feeling of being fully present.*

And here is one more paradox, while we are at it. Sometimes the way we can bring the most energy and presence to any relationship with another Being is by realizing that we sometimes have to take time and space away from that relationship so that we can be more fully present when we are together.

Before you burn this book in protest, spend a little time thinking about this. Do you think you can be most present for your significant other at the end of a long, stressful week at work, when you walk in the door, exhausted, sleep-deprived, energetically-drained, and grouchy because of all of the demands of others, or when you return from a day of hiking where you had been in the peace and solitude of nature, recharging your own emotional batteries?

My wife and I would likely not be married today had it not been for a three-week trip to Ecuador in 2009. There were a number of reasons that trip saved our marriage, but the most important was that it removed all of the competing distractions for the emotional energy that we each had been dedicating to relationships outside our marriage. Both our jobs were taking a tremendous amount of emotional energy, and very little was coming into our relationship. We were burning the proverbial candle at both ends, not taking care of our Physical or Spiritual selves. During our three weeks away, we spent many days together, but we also took some days for individual activities. This gave us time to reconnect with who we were as individuals and then allowed us to have the emotional energy to reconnect as a couple and remember and see again the person we each fell in love with.

I want to be clear that I am not suggesting that recharging your emotional energy requires a three-week trip disconnected from all of the distractions of everyday life, but if you can do that, I highly recommend it. It can be as simple as a fifteen-minute walk outside at lunch, five minutes of meditation, or a weekly massage. It can be a series of small things done consistently that recharge your emotional batteries. However, I do think it has to be something that you do just for you, and you must acknowledge to yourself that you are taking time for yourself.

I also believe there are some times in life when a more substantial period of emotional recharge is necessary. There are times when five minutes of meditation or a walk at lunch are just not going to do it. If your proverbial oxygen mask has indeed fallen from the ceiling, you might need a day, a long weekend, a week, or even a month of time to focus on and care for yourself. As I said before, most of us think that we are selfish when we take this time, when, in fact, we are selfish not to.

I learned and experienced this lesson most vividly at a couple's retreat hosted by Philip and Pauline McKernan. Through their couple's work, they emphasize that we are individuals first, and we bring how we are as individuals into the relationship. By taking time to nurture our individual needs, we then have the ability to show up more fully in our relationship. They believe time alone, exploring and recharging emotional energy, is critical to a healthy relationship, so critical that they build this time into their family schedule. Again, this seems counterintuitive, but remember, it is a paradox. In order to be fully physically and emotionally present with another Being, you must spend some time away from them.

HOW TO LOVE

Zen Master Thich Nhat Hanh, in his book *How to Love,* shares the analogy of our individual love as being like a home.[7] He says that our true home is inside each one of us and that when we are in a loving relationship, we are sharing our home with another. Once we understand that our true home is inside of us, then we can open our home to another. However, if we do not take care of our true home, the home inside of us, then we will only have our own pain and suffering to share with the other, which is no gift to share at all. By taking care of ourselves and taking the time we need to get

---

7   Thicht Nhất Hạnh, *How to Love* (California: Parallax Press, 2014).

our own home in order, we will have a loving, warm home to share with the other people in our lives.

Another benefit of time away from both objects and Beings in our environment is that distance can provide clarity on how we feel about those objects or Beings. Remember, every thing, object, or Being in our environment emits energy. It has a vibration. While we are in the presence of that vibration, we are feeling the effects and are under its influence, so to speak. Sometimes, being in close proximity and feeling this vibration and energy can be clarifying. We need to touch an object, feel the energy of the other Being, to know how it makes us feel. Other times, we can gain more clarity by not being in the energetic presence of the Being or object. For example, when my wife and I moved to a smaller space, we went through our possessions and gave some away, but we also put some in boxes and are storing them. I can't remember exactly what is in those boxes, but at the time, it was all important enough that I felt I had to keep it. It has been two years, and I haven't needed a single thing from those boxes. I now have much more clarity about those objects and how important they are to my day-to-day happiness and well-being.

On the surface, it may sound callous to say that an absence from the people in your life can serve the same purpose, but that doesn't make it any less true. If you are unclear how you feel about the person you have been dating for a few months or the person you have been married to for twenty years, spend a week or a month away from them on your own. As you have the time away, check in with your emotions and feelings periodically. Are you enjoying your time away but anxious to see them again, or are you sad to see your time away gradually coming to an end? Do you find yourself physically and emotionally missing them? When you walk in the door after being gone for a week or a month, do you fill with happiness and joy, or is there a different emotion? The brutal truth is that you do not serve anyone by not being honest about your feelings and emotions. The other Being in a relationship deserves to know how you feel. We are being selfish by not sharing our feelings.

We are often guilty of creating a Story that we think protects another Being and saves them from emotional pain by not sharing how we feel. In reality, we are depriving them of their power when we could either allow them to choose to do something differently or allow them to choose a different relationship if this one is not working. If I had to sum up this entire discussion in one sentence, it would be this: *our obligation in every relationship is to honestly express how we feel, and it is up to the other person how they react.* We have to be willing to accept their reaction.

Sure, there are nuances to this statement, but it is far less nuanced than you would imagine. If you are not happy after one year in a relationship and don't tell the other person and spend the next twenty years in an unhappy relationship, not ever being fully present, you have taken the possibility of twenty years of happiness away from the other person by not sharing your true feelings, and that is selfish. If your spouse doesn't pick the bath mat up and it drives you crazy, you carry that negative energy into other aspects of your relationship without them knowing why. That is selfish.

It doesn't always have to be negative feelings that you have to share. It is just as important to share positive feelings as well. In the past, I have not done a great job of sharing words of affirmation or gratitude with my wife. If you rarely tell them how much you love them or all the things you are grateful for, then how are they supposed to know? Tell the Beings in your life you love them, you appreciate them, and how grateful you are for having them in your life. Not sharing your positive feelings is selfish, too.

CHAPTER 13

MENTORS

As I mentioned earlier, poems come to me when an event or place has inspired something within me at such a deep level that I am moved to try and capture the essence of the experience. I wrote this poem in May 2018, after a two-day retreat called BraveMind with Philip McKernan. Mentors can work in numerous ways, ranging from creating subtle shifts in your perception of your current reality, to completely cracking open your head and heart. In this two-day retreat, Philip cracked my way of thinking and feeling open. As any great mentor can do, he showed me a glimpse of what was possible and then gave me the little nudge I needed.

THERE IS A LAND I KNOW

There is a land I know,
for I have walked its hills and valleys many times.
I was born here.
I have spent all my days here.

Sometimes I see a new bird, find a new tree,
but most things are familiar, comfortable.
Except for the cliff.
Sometimes I walk to the cliff, but it is always misty and foggy,
And I can never see what lies beyond.

One day while I was standing on the cliff, looking,
a stranger appeared.
I was not alarmed, for I felt no danger from him.
He came and stood beside me.
I asked him if he knew what was beyond the cliff.

He looked over the edge.
He saw the same mist and fog that I had always seen.
He looked at me and said, "Only one way to find out."
And he pushed me.

As discussed earlier, there are only two external ways in which we learn anything as Beings:

1. Through what we experience directly.
2. Through what we are told, taught, or shown by others.

Mentors are extremely important because, at a basic level, they show us and help us determine the stories or Egoic Interpretations that we create around the Life Events that happen in our lives. As we know, the Egoic Interpretation of the Life Event contributes to who we are.

For human beings, the first mentors in our world are typically our parents. Think about a baby experiencing the world for the first time. The baby is taught the social norms of society by its parents. As the child grows and experiences new things and new social interactions, they look to their parents to see how to react to the new situations. It used to be, before the internet, a person only knew what was possible by what they saw around them as an example. In the good sense of the word, a mentor gives you a new perspective and expands your view, your Story, of what is even possible for yourself. Humans are classic at selling ourselves short or at least allowing society to keep us from being our highest and best selves, whatever that means. In reality, there is very little you can't do once you know or think something is possible. A good mentor expands your view as to what is possible.

One point to consider is that we generally view the word mentor in the positive, but remember the opposite side of the coin is just as powerful and is the downfall of many potentially awesome lives. Just as a good mentor can change your life for the positive, the wrong mentor can be a huge negative influence in your life. If you learn how to interact with the world through a mentor, and you learn poor habits and hear and see the negative side of the world, well, the effects can ruin your life. Many of our great thinkers have touched on this point in one form or another: Napoleon Hill, Ben Franklin, Einstein, etc.

One of the most important decisions you make is choosing who serves as your mentors, and most people don't even consciously make this decision. Think about how the wrong mentor can destroy a life. If the example you have and the language you hear is about *why it can't be done* or that *the deck is stacked against you*, or *that's how it is for people like us*, that is a very tough place to be in. If your example of success is making it through the day so you can drink at the bar each night, well, you can see where that ends.

AWARENESS

So much of what we are talking about comes back to awareness. Most people are not even aware of who the people are in their lives that are acting as mentors. Make no mistake, you have them; it's just a question of determining who they are and then choosing who you want them to be. Once you are aware that you can choose for someone to be a mentor, then you are in control. It is a simple switch to flip, but most of us are not even aware the switch exists. Look at the people in your life who currently influence or have influenced and acted as an example in your life.

Make a list of all these people right now down the left side of a piece of paper. On the right side of the page, start a column heading with +/−. Now bring each person into your mind and then decide if they are/were a positive influence, a negative influence, or possibly a bit of both. There are people in our lives who can have a positive influence but then also have some beliefs or values that you don't want to carry as part of you. Mark them as +/−. If we are honest, often our parents fall into the +/− category. There is no judgment around this. It makes perfect sense. Most of us spent the most formative years of our lives with our parents. We were around them twenty-four hours a day, seven days a week, 365 days a year. We saw the good and the bad. We learned what we liked in our parents and what we didn't.

Sometimes just the simple act of realizing that someone was a mentor, in the sense of having an influence in your life, and then becoming aware that you do not want to recreate their Story or life is all you need to change the Story. Knowing how or what you *do not want to be* can be just as important as knowing how or what *you want to be*. Sometimes the greatest lessons come from people we do not want to be like.

To be clear, your life has been influenced or changed by *every* person that you've met. The right mentors can absolutely change your life, and the relationship doesn't have to be with someone you meet in person, or who is even living for that matter. A lesson can be taught in many ways. If you have access to books or the internet, then you have access to mentors. Here is a great way to think about it. Look around your life, and think of the people in your community, books you have read, videos you have seen, or talks you have listened to and consider whose behavior you have been inspired by or who you would like to be like in a certain situation. Think about phrases like: "I would like to be more like _____ when it comes to _____" or "I respect _____ for the way they handled _____." Then start studying those people in those situations. Figure out how they developed their mindset. Who have they looked up to? Often, just understanding their Story and why they think the way they do will change how you approach the world and change *you*. The key is being aware of who you are choosing as a mentor and why you are choosing that person.

BELIEFS

The mentors in our life are important for a number of reasons, but one of the most important things that great mentors do is to affirm and reinforce beliefs that serve us, and challenge the beliefs that no longer serve us. Two types of beliefs that do not serve us are limiting beliefs and blocking beliefs. As with many situations, awareness is the key to identifying these beliefs, so let's discuss them here.

We all come into this world with infinite possibility, then Life Events and Egoic Interpretations begin to stack up and create our belief system. Our belief system shapes how we see the world and, most importantly, what we believe is possible and impossible. Certain Life Events that happen, when combined with their Egoic Interpretation, can create a limiting belief or a blocking belief.

A limiting belief creates a limit on what you think could be possible. A limiting belief is something like, *I could speak to five people, but I could never speak to five hundred or five thousand,* or *I could run a mile, but I could never run a marathon,* or, *I can sing in the shower, but I could never sing on a stage.*

A blocking belief is much more insidious. *A blocking belief blocks you from even considering that the object of your belief is possible to such an extent that it becomes a subconscious default.* It becomes: I can't be a speaker, I am not a runner, I can't sing, and therefore, you never even consider the possibility of even attempting it. You never even try.

The thing about beliefs is that they all originate from somewhere. We were not born into this world with any beliefs. A Life Event happened, all of our previous Life Events and Egoic Interpretations were taken into account, and we created a belief around the Story. Certain combinations of Life Events and Egoic Interpretations can be intense enough that they cause a blocking belief. In many cases, these blocking beliefs don't even originate from knowledge that happened to us but come from knowledge told to us by others. For example, someone may have said, "Nobody in our family has the body type to run. We are just not runners." So, when asked if you are a runner, the blocking belief kicks in, and the default answer is no.

"Why not?"

"Well, nobody in my family is a runner. We don't have the body type, so we don't run."

"Have you tried it?"

"No."

No firsthand knowledge. All based on the knowledge of others.

Blocking beliefs are often at the root cause of prejudices as well. A child grows up hearing, "We don't like purple people." "Purple people are bad people." "Purple people are mean." "Purple people will steal from you." "You can't trust purple people."

As an adult, the person is asked, "Do you like Purple people?" And the response is, "No. They are bad people. They will steal from you."

"Oh, has a Purple person stolen from you?"

"No."

"Have you met any Purple people?"

"No."

"Have you been to where Purple people live?"

"No."

There has never been a challenge to this blocking belief.

LIMITING AND BLOCKING BELIEFS ARE DREAM KILLERS

And now we come to it. I believe that limiting and blocking beliefs are dream killers and are responsible for a tremendous amount of suffering in this world. A bold statement, but think about it for a moment. If you are struggling with the question of what you are meant to do, I believe either a limiting belief or a blocking belief is keeping you from answering that question.

I struggled with that question for *forty-two years.*

I had some very dark periods in my life when I felt like a failure because I didn't know what I was meant to do. And when I say dark, I mean depression. I mean waking up each morning and dreading the start of the day because it represented another round of struggle just to make it through the day. It meant feeling run down and low on energy because nothing excited me. It meant my relationship with my wife and friends suffered because I was in a dark mood or short-tempered. It meant feeling like I was in a very long, dark tunnel with no light at the other end.

What makes it even worse is that, by all accounts, I had done everything right, and I should have been happy. I studied hard, got good grades, and went to graduate school. I graduated and landed a coveted full-time, permanent job with the federal government, which had always been my goal. I was working with a great group of people in one of the "top cities to live" in the United States. I was married to a beautiful woman who had a thriving career of her own. I was healthy and had a great group of friends.

Based on my belief system growing up, I had arrived. And yet, I was not happy. Not even close. I could not shake the feeling that there should be something more. I should be excited about my life, but life felt like a chore. How could this possibly be? What was wrong with me? By all standards, by my standards, I had achieved my goals, and I should be living a great life. What was wrong with me? Why couldn't I just be happy? I beat myself up for not being able to figure out why I was not happy.

I would try and rally myself out of my unhappiness using logic. I would rationalize that I had accomplished my goals, and I had so much to be thankful for, especially in a world where I had so much more than others. I should be happy with what I had. Not being happy seemed self-indulgent, almost embarrassing, especially when there were many people, including family or friends, that would have happily traded places and taken my steady government job with guaranteed raises and yearly vacation increases. I should have been set for life. And this just made me feel even more unhappy. And this gets to the core of why blocking beliefs are so insidious and destructive in our lives. Because no matter how hard you look or search for something, if there is a blocking belief in place, you can never find the answer because your conscious mind does not even see the answer as a possibility and never even considers it. *And what makes blocking beliefs so dangerous is that you don't even know you have them, but that is about to change.*

In hindsight, I can see the blocking belief that was causing me so much unhappiness and depression and understand its origins. I was raised by a single mother who achieved her professional success in life through education, so education was very important. My mother always said I could be anything I wanted to be, but I always saw that through the lens of higher education. The road out of the small town I grew up in was education. She was also a high school principal, and everyone we socialized with was a teacher. My father was also a teacher, so all of my career examples showed getting an education and then finding a reliable, salaried job. Sure, the pay may be low, but you have a steady salary and a guaranteed retirement. When people were being laid off at the local factories, you would still have a job, and after thirty years, you would have a pension. You would never be rich, but you would have food on the table. Ironically enough, you also didn't have to be happy in your job either. I knew plenty of teachers who did not enjoy teaching, but I also knew some who did. My view of a successful career was stable, salaried, and came with a pension. You probably were not going to be happy every day doing it, but at least you would have benefits, a salary, and a good retirement in thirty years.

Fast forward to 2009. I had a few years in my full-time, permanent position with the United States Department of Agriculture. I had a good salary, good benefits, and a solid retirement plan with twenty-six more years of work to go. I got four weeks of paid vacation a year and all the federal holidays. I had invested four years in undergraduate, three years in grad school, and two years in a position to build my resume, all to land a full-time position with the government. I had finally arrived, and I was miserable. How could this possibly be? How could I not be happy?

GOLDEN HANDCUFFS

And this brings us to the partner of blocking beliefs: golden handcuffs. Blocking beliefs and golden handcuffs make quite a team to keep us in unhappy places. Think of golden handcuffs as the things that we feel we will be giving up if we make a change. My salary was a golden handcuff, the benefits were a golden handcuff, the stable job was a golden handcuff. And the biggest golden handcuff of all was the nearly ten years of education and resume building work I had invested in getting this job. How could I walk away from all of this when I couldn't even figure out what else I might want to do? The answer for me was that I couldn't. Remember, one of my beliefs was that more education was always the answer. So, this was the point where I tried to solve the problem with education once more. I enrolled in an evening MBA program and spent the next two years working at a job I didn't like during the day and getting my MBA during the evenings and on weekends.

I used a personal example related to a blocking belief around my career because I think so many people are struggling in this area, but remember, you can have a blocking belief in any area of your life. If you ever use the words "I can't" or "I could never," these could be an indication of a blocking belief.

At this point, maybe you are nodding along and saying, *I think I have some blocking beliefs, and I definitely have those golden handcuffs, but I have kids and bills and obligations. I can't just throw all of that away in hopes of finding something I really like. I have a lot of time and energy invested.*

You are right, and I am not asking you to quit your job tomorrow, sell everything, and spend the next twelve months on a soul-searching pilgrimage around the world. However, I am asking you to get curious about your blocking beliefs and at least try to identify what they may be. The truth is that some of you are not ready to uncover your blocking beliefs, and you will find a way to gloss over this whole concept. Our conscious brain and our ego try to protect us from truths that could be painful or challenge the status quo. I understand that, and if this is you and you're starting to skim or gloss over this section, then think about it again. Hit pause on your ego, and if you still can't get into the notion of blocking beliefs, that's okay. You are just not ready. Keep this book around and visit it in a year or two. Maybe the idea will land with you then, and you will be ready.

For some of you, this exploration may be easy. In fact, maybe just reading this section and realizing that there is such a thing as blocking beliefs has allowed you to identify yours. Maybe the light bulb has already gone off, and you realize that this corporate law job is not what you are meant to do. You can admit to yourself that all you have ever wanted to be is a baker. You can picture the cottage on Vashon Island that you will turn into your bakery. The weathered, cedar shingles covering the exterior, the large wood fire oven inside. You will bake sourdoughs and rustic loaves, and every Thursday, you will host community night, where all the locals will gather for wood-fired pizza. You will build a community around your bakery and weave yourself into the local fabric. You will be happy rising at four o'clock each morning to start the baking for the day and go to bed each night satisfied with a day well spent.

For others, like me, a blocking belief can be much harder to uncover. I have struggled mightily to uncover mine for years, in fact. I am sure I still have others that I am not even aware of yet. But I can promise you from personal experience that the rewards of uncovering your blocking beliefs can be nothing short of life-changing.

If you are struggling, here are a few questions you can start to work with that could point towards your blocking beliefs:

1. Is there anything I think about doing but then say, "I can't do that" or "I could never do that?"
2. Has a friend or family member asked you, "Have you ever thought about being...?" or "Have you ever thought about doing...?"
3. If you could do anything you wanted to for work, and money was no concern, what would you do?
4. If you could be instantly good at a sport or hobby, what would it be?
5. Fill in the following blank: every time I talk to _____, what he/she does sounds so interesting. I think I would enjoy doing that.

Since blocking beliefs are often something we can't see ourselves, another great tool for identifying them is getting help from others. What can be a little tricky is that sometimes those closest to us are the ones responsible for creating or solidifying our blocking belief in the first place. This is not meant as a criticism. It is reality. This should not stop you from getting help from others, though; just be aware of it as you discuss this topic with them. Often, our friends and family see aspects of us that we can't see or remember things about us that we have consciously forgotten.

For example, you might want to ask your parents if there was a sport or activity that you were really good at or enjoyed doing as a child that you don't do anymore. Maybe you loved to draw or paint as a child, but you haven't picked up a paintbrush in years. Maybe you loved to go camping or hiking or splash in a creek, and now you live in a city and haven't slept in a tent for decades. On the flip side, if your parents have been telling you that you were born to be a doctor since you were three years old, they might not be the ones to ask about occupations.

People that don't know you very well, especially more recent acquaintances with whom you don't have much history, can also be a good source of identifying blocking beliefs. Sometimes you have short but intense relationships with people. For example, my wife and I went on a cycling trip in Vietnam. We met twelve other people from around the world and spent morning, noon, and night with them for the next ten days. We dined together, rode bikes together, toured ancient temples together, and had a few sweaty, smelly bus rides together. We also had lots of conversations throughout. Sometimes, when you expect you will never see someone again, more of who you are can shine through. And it doesn't have to be on a bike trip halfway around the world. It could be at a business conference in a different city or maybe just in an evening spent around a campfire with new friends. But if you are ever having a conversation in this type of situation and hear the words, "That surprises me, you seem like the type of person that would be great at..." or "I would have never guessed that based on what I know about you." In conversations, these are bread crumbs, so pay attention.

If you have read this far and it still feels totally hopeless, and as much as you want it to be different and feel different, you feel even more desperate and overwhelmed and lost than you did before, then you are exactly who I am writing this book for. I have been there, and I am writing about all of these things from experience. The reason it is so hard for you is that you have a blocking belief that is so ingrained in you that you can't even consider what might possibly make your heart light up. There is no simple, easy three-step process that can uncover it. It is going to take work. Take a serious look at all of the variables of the Being Equation. Do the exercises, dig into your past Life Events, analyze the people and objects in your environment, and get help from others to figure out who you are first. Change the stories you are telling yourself.

Once you know who you are, the blocking belief will have no power over you.

What I am giving you is hope and assurance that something different is possible if you dig in and don't give up. I am not going to blow sunshine here. I said it was possible. I didn't say it was going to be easy. I have been in those dark places myself, and when I was in the darkest places, I had no hope. I am telling you right now; it can be different. The world deserves to see the amazing, powerful Being that you are, even if you don't believe it yet yourself.

Keep digging, and you will.

The leg that you have up now is that you know that there is such a thing as a blocking belief. You know that if you can find out what yours is, your life can change. For my first forty-two years, I didn't know that something like blocking beliefs could exist, and it has not been until recently that I learned the concept. I just continued to beat myself up because, no matter how hard I tried, I could not figure out what I was meant to do.

A mentor of mine, Larry Kendall, teaches that people ultimately make decisions for one of two reasons, to alleviate pain or to induce pleasure. You will finally make a decision when the pain of not doing something becomes intense enough, or there is the reward of pleasure. Until either pain or pleasure reaches the tipping point, you will keep kicking the proverbial decision can down the road and maintain the status quo. For me, pain was the reason for my change.

The pain of going to a job day after day, week after week, month after month, got so bad that I could no longer do it. I knew I was physically present at my job but putting in about 10 percent of the effort I was capable of contributing, and no matter how hard I tried, I just couldn't make it work. It was greatly affecting my physical and emotional health and was a huge weight on the relationships in my life I cared most about, so I left the stable, salaried job I had invested fourteen years of time and energy to achieve, and part of me felt like a failure because I still had the blocking belief that was driving my thinking.

I didn't know what the blocking belief was then, but I can put words to it now because, in hindsight, I can see exactly why I struggled so mightily to leave that job. My blocking belief was that I had to have a steady, salaried job with benefits to be safe and secure. Leaving this job, one that is about as high on the stable spectrum as you can go, went against nearly every piece of knowledge and belief that I had around what represented a successful occupation. I did feel a sense of relief deep within me when I made the decision to make the change, but there was also a sense of fear. I wish I could say that after my last day at that job, I had a renewed sense of excitement and direction and things in my life fell right into place, but that is not the case. I also didn't make the decision to leave one day and then walk out the door the next. As I mentioned, I spent two years getting an MBA, thinking that would open the door to even more stable, salaried jobs. Little did I know that it would not be the case. I could have never foreseen the path before me and how I have ultimately ended up where I am more than a decade later, but here I am, living a life I could have never dreamed possible, as happy as I have ever been, with no salaried job, no benefits, and no pension.

Did I have the epiphany about my blocking belief a decade ago? No. It was only after I made changes in my life that I could look back and see the blocking beliefs that were holding me back from my happiness. The life that I have now, the work that I do, my current lifestyle could never be possible in a stable, salaried position. What I do now is 180 degrees from my government job, and it is something I would never have considered in the realm of possibility.

I have said it before, but it is worth restating, *blocking beliefs are so insidious because they eliminate the answer to your question from the realm of consideration before you even start looking.* Why was it not in consideration? Since what I do now has no guaranteed salary, or stability, or benefits, or pension, I could have never dreamt of it as a possibility. I own my own business. I am an entrepreneur. I created something new and novel that did not exist, and I built a business around it.

So how did I make it to where I am today?

I wish I could tell you that I awoke one morning and realized this is exactly what I needed to do, but that was not the case. Sometimes as individuals, we can see the decisions we need to make, and then the responsibility becomes ours to make them. Other times, the universe has to give us a nudge, so to speak, and make some decisions for us. I took my new shiny MBA and started applying for jobs. I thought with two master's degrees, an extensive resume of work in the public, private, and education sectors, and excellent reference letters that I would have no problem finding a new job. I applied for numerous positions, sending out over sixty resumes over the course of a few months. I got a single interview and no job. Nothing makes you feel more like a failure than doing exactly what you thought you should do, getting plenty of education, building a solid history of work experience, keeping a clean cut-image and profile, and then proceeding to get rejected for months on end.

SO, WHAT DID I DO?

I went into real estate because I had a real estate license, and they would accept me.

I have always enjoyed real estate, but I never pictured myself involved in real estate sales. I am the furthest thing from a salesperson. I hate to shop for cars because of car "salespeople," and here I was, a newly minted real estate broker. Luckily for me, I landed at the one real estate company in the world where I could thrive, The Group, Inc., in Northern Colorado. My real estate career began by attending a four-day workshop taught by a man who would become a great mentor to me, Larry Kendall.

Larry developed a real estate sales system called Ninja, and the Ninja System has drastically changed my life. I believe that the Ninja System is really a personal development system couched in the context of real estate. Despite all of my previous education, I was introduced to new concepts through Ninja that I had never heard before, and the impact of this knowledge was profound. Among other things, Larry taught us how the brain works, the power of gratitude and affirmations, and how to build relationships. He exposed me to the entire field of personal development and writers like Napoleon Hill, Zig Ziglar, Tony Robbins, etc. I began to understand that our brain is not just the control center for us as humans on a scientific level but also learned how our thoughts control us.

My mind was blown. The book you are reading now is the result of the seeds planted in those first few days of Larry's teachings. It started me on a decadelong exploration of personal development that led me to read hundreds of books, spend time journaling and meditating, and exploring Spirituality and the mind with works by Eckhart Tolle, Paohlo Coelho, Thich Naht Hahn, Michael Singer, Deepak Chopra, Oprah, and Sadghuru, among others. Podcasters and writers like Tim Ferris, Rich Roll, Michael Pollan, and many more as well as the guests they hosted, were also sources of influence. I have spent literally thousands of hours reading and consuming the content of these writers and podcasters, and, while not a formal education, I consider my education here every bit as important as the two master's degrees I received through university training. The level of work and time investment in researching and learning in this field has been far greater than my time and investment in the university.

Three years ago, I met Philip McKernan, and my work with him changed my life. I began to work with Philip because some of the things he said resonated with something deep within me. I had never had a formal mentoring or coaching relationship before, and I was, frankly, skeptical that I would receive value that would offset the financial cost. I decided to give it a try. As I have said before, sometimes we need someone from the outside to see what is obvious but that we can't see ourselves.

Philip has an incredible ability to see the little threads within us to tug on, and when he starts tugging, he can unravel the whole paradigm you have built in your mind. I believe Philip is a master at identifying the Life Events and their Egoic Interpretations that are dominating our lives by creating limiting and blocking beliefs. Philip can see a little spark deep within someone and then fan it, just so, to turn it into a roaring flame. He will be the first to say that he doesn't do anything but shine a light on what is possible for each of us to do for ourselves. Through working with Philip and a lot of individual work on my own, I realized I was not showing up fully in this world. I was keeping part of myself walled away, playing it safe, pleasing everyone around me, and not ever asking what I wanted for myself. Although he doesn't use these words, he helped me uncover the past Life Events and the Egoic Interpretations that were controlling my life. He showed me that I had something to offer the world. He told me to be brave and that I matter.

I have also been part of a mastermind with members from all around the country for the past five years. The people I have met, the speakers I have heard, and the examples of people living lives beyond the ordinary have all shown me what is possible, just like the example of Roger Bannister breaking the four-minute mile. Once you see it can be done and that the people who have done it are real, with faults and flaws just like you or me, then the barriers in your mind start to crumble.

About a year ago, I was also involved in starting a local mastermind. It is a group of ten guys who get together once a month and share what is going well in their lives. We also share our challenges. We support each other, give advice, and just listen. Most of us don't see each other regularly outside of this monthly meeting, but when we come together, we genuinely care about and support one another, which is something that is generally lacking in our hyper-connected social world. You cannot replace genuine in-person connections.

I tell you all of these things because I know I personally could never have gone on this journey of discovering who I am alone. The irony is that to answer the question: *who am I?* you will need help from others on the outside. As the Being Equation shows, every person and every thing we interact with shapes who we are. Without the influence of so many others, I would not be the person I am today.

As I have said, I could never have foreseen the life I have today ten years ago. I don't have any new licenses or credentials or certifications, but I have lived every word of this discovery journey. I have personally experienced everything I have shared with you. I have twenty years of science and fifteen years of Spiritual and personal development and a lifetime of personal experience that has brought me to this moment where I can share the Being Equation with you. I wrote this because I don't want another person to struggle one more day with questions about who they are and what they are meant to do. I know the pain and suffering that struggle causes, and I hope what I have learned can help you.

In the remaining chapters, we will discuss the practical application of the Being Equation: what you should do now, how to take this knowledge and apply it to yourself, and how to use this knowledge to understand who you are and who you want to be.

The truth is that most of us are scared of shining too brightly, of being our highest and best self. We all say that is what we want, but then the doubt creeps in, and we worry about what our family and friends will think. If I get famous, become really successful, or build a life in which I am content and happy, what will they think? Will my growth and development be accepted and celebrated by those I love, or will it scare them? Will they be inspired by my changes, or will they be resentful because it shines a little light on their own choice to not be their highest and best selves? I can't answer that question for you, and I imagine there will be some of both in your life when you start on this journey.

That it is not your responsibility or burden to bear. Your purpose is to live your highest and best life and to share your gifts with the world. Your responsibility is to do just that, and if someone is not happy with you for doing that or feels threatened or overshadowed by your personal growth, then that is their journey. I implore you, do not play small to keep those around you comfortable. You are doing yourself and the world a disservice. By all means, invite them along, lift those around you up, too, show up fully in this world, and share your gifts. Give those around you the opportunity to grow through you and your experience, and many will. But remember, if they don't, that is not on you.

CHAPTER 14

APPLYING THE BEING EQUATION

We have come to a very exciting part of the book for me, personally. You have invested time and energy into learning the fundamental building blocks of the Being Equation, and now it is time to put it to use to start changing your life. In this chapter, you will learn how to apply the Being Equation by walking through two examples, and then the next chapter will discuss some specific exercises you can use to explore each variable in the Being Equation in more depth as it relates to your own life.

In numerous places throughout this book, I have mentioned the Being Equation is time-dependent, meaning it defines exactly who you are at a discrete moment in time, (t). Pardon me while I geek out for just one minute because this concept is unbelievably exciting to me, and it is crucial in understanding how to use the full power of the Being Equation. What this means is that you can use the Being Equation to take a snapshot and see exactly who you were at any moment in time from the past and up to this exact present moment. Where it gets really exciting to me, is how you can then use the Being Equation as a tool to create the Being you would like to be in the future.

To apply the Being Equation, start with the First Principles that the Being Equation defines:

1. Your body is a combination of the Spiritual and Physical.
2. Your body needs both Spiritual and Physical Inputs to survive and thrive.
3. Every Being and object in your environment affect who you are.
4. Every Life Event and Egoic Interpretation of the Life Event is creating who you are in the present moment.

You are creating the Being you are by what you consume and the environment in which you live (Inputs), the experiences you have (Life Events), and the stories you create from those experiences (Egoic Interpretation). Your life is your creation.

Remember, you are a powerful creator because you come from the ultimate creative power, Source Energy. You are here solely to create an experience called "your life." The life you create is up to you. The Being Equation shows you how to create the life you want to have.

The Being Equation defines a Being at any moment in time, so the easiest way to use it is to compare your current state to whatever state you would like to create, and then identify what changes you need to make to move from the present to that future state.

The Being Equation is so powerful because you can apply it to any duration of time as a tool to understand why you were the Being you were in that moment. The time and depth of reflection may vary depending on the length of time frame you are examining, but the process is still the same.

1. Write out the Being Equation, and reflect on your current situation for each variable.
2. Look at the past, and see how your choices have brought you to this present moment.
3. Update the equation so that the final result is the Being you want to be.
4. Identify what variables need to change to move you forward to become the Being you want to be.

Let's walk through two examples for two different time durations to see how this is done at a practical level.

Example one:

Pretend you are sitting at your desk in your office. It is Wednesday afternoon at two o'clock, and you have a big project due Monday morning. You have been working sixteen-hour days for the last week and even worked through the weekend and missed out on time with your husband and children. You haven't exercised in a week, and you are feeling incredibly scattered and stressed. You don't feel like you are making any forward progress at all. You have four days until this project is due, but you don't have any idea how to get from here to there, and you are overwhelmed. How are you going to go from the tired, frazzled, stressed Being you are now to the type of Being you need to be to get this project done?

Use the Being Equation to take stock of who you are now and how to get to where you want to be. Write out each variable for the present moment:

$$B_x(t) = f(SPIL_xE_x)$$

(t) = **Time:** The present moment.

S = **Spirit:** I am completely drained, and I know that I really need to do something to recharge. I usually do a yoga class twice a week or go for a walk in the park over lunch, but I haven't done either in over a week.

P = **Physical Body:** I usually do five minutes of stretching as soon as I get out of bed each morning, but I haven't even done that this past week. The yoga and walks are also good for my Physical Body, and those have gone out the window. My body feels tired and sluggish.

I = **Inputs:** Since I have been spending so much time at work, I have been grabbing takeout and foraging for whatever is in the break room. I have also been having a late afternoon coffee, which has been making it harder to sleep the last few nights. The office lights and extended time in front of a computer screen are not good either.

L_x = **Life Events:** All Life Events have been dominated by work. When I do go home, I am too tired to spend real time with my husband or children. All I want to do is crawl in bed.

E_x = **Egoic Interpretation:** Hard work is the only way to get ahead. I remember many evenings and weekends when my father missed dinner or wasn't there for my games on Saturday because of work. If you want to get ahead, this is just the way it is.

Is this the life you want at this moment, or do you want to create something different? Use the Being Equation to do it. Ask yourself what you can change to create a different you.

(t) = **Time:** The very near future.

S = **Spirit:** I feel drained, but I know there is a yoga class at three o'clock in the afternoon, and I have my yoga clothes in a duffel bag in the car. If I leave work in the next thirty minutes, I can make the class. It would be so good for my Spirit to do some yoga. My brain will be recharged when I sit down to work again.

P = **Physical Body:** I can feel my body getting excited and energized by the simple thought of yoga, and I know the stretching and moving for an hour would be great for it.

I = **Inputs:** There happens to be a restaurant right next to the yoga studio that specializes in healthy, organic meals. I have taken home meals from there before, and my family really enjoys them. That would be the perfect dinner to have this evening.

L_x = **Life Events:** I haven't been home before eight o'clock in the evening this past week, and I know my husband and children miss me. I am going to call my husband right now and tell him I will be home at five o'clock and that I will bring dinner with me. I am also going to invite him and the children on a family walk after dinner.

E_x = **Egoic Interpretation:** Why do I have this belief that working hard has to always be equated with sacrificing my health and time with my family? As I think back on the memories of my father, I wonder if this idea about work is one I want to have. Is it really serving me? Where does this fear come from that, if I don't work every minute between now and Monday morning, the project will fail? And why is it controlling me? Deep down, I know I can get this project done; it's that I am not thinking straight right now because I am burned out at the moment. I know I will be ten times more effective after a bit of recharge.

You shut your computer down for the day and head to yoga. You finish yoga and Spiritually and physically already feel better and more grounded. You have dinner with your family and spend an hour sitting at the table and talking and laughing. After dinner, you walk around the neighborhood and have time and energy for a tuck-in and bedtime story with the kids. For the first time in a week, your head is not spinning, and you actually feel relaxed.

You get to work the next morning and get more done in a few hours than all of the last two days combined. You realize that maybe you don't have to burn the candle at both ends and sacrifice your Spiritual and physical health and time with your family to be successful at your job. Now you have a new Life Event and Egoic Interpretation to call on, and maybe it is time to really challenge some of those stories around work from your past so you can create your future.

Example two:

Pretend it is the morning of your fortieth birthday. Your head is a bit bleary from one too many drinks the night before. You walk to the bathroom and catch a glimpse of yourself in the mirror and don't like what you see. When did your belly get so big? You make a cup of coffee and jump in the shower to get dressed for a job you don't find exciting. Your wife is up and already off to work as she had an early meeting and will be working late again tonight. The past two years have been pretty stressful as you have each been focusing on your careers and not each other. If you're being honest, you have drifted a little bit apart because you don't spend much time together.

You get to the office and open your email to find an inbox overflowing with messages. Your mood moves from one of general disappointment with the day to one of downright dread. You trudge through another day at work and walk in the door at six o'clock in the evening to an empty house.

There you sit, on your fortieth birthday at a job you don't like, in a marriage that needs some attention, and in a body that is about thirty pounds overweight. You know that it took years to get to this place, and it is going to take some time to change it, but you are committed to starting to change it right now, so you pull out a sheet of paper and start by writing down the Being Equation and working through the variables.

$$B_x(t) = f(SPIL_xE_x)$$

(t) = **Time:** The present moment.

S = **Spirit:** My Spirit is feeling really low. I used to go for hikes in the mountains or go fly fishing and camping, and I haven't done anything like that in over a year. I had also been good about writing in my journal and even creating the occasional poem or story. I don't even know where my journal is these days.

P = **Physical Body:** If I am honest, I am embarrassed by my Physical Body at the moment. I used to run and bike at least five times per week, but over the last year, I am lucky if I get out once a month. I probably have thirty pounds of flab that is making me feel very bad about my physical self.

I = **Inputs:** I really don't enjoy the neighborhood where we live. We bought the house two years ago, and it seemed like a good move at the time. It was a bigger house in a nicer neighborhood, and I thought the extra space would be good for us. It turns out we don't have any friends in this area, and it is a twenty-minute drive to our friends' houses or the restaurants we like. This house also costs a lot more on a monthly basis than I thought it would, and that is bringing lots of stress to the marriage.

I am also eating poorly and drinking too much at night. I drink to try and get my mind off the stress and then end up making some poor food choices. This is very different from how it used to be when I was training for a half marathon.

L_x = **Life Events:** Where do I even start with this one? The majority of Life Events throughout my day are things I have to do instead of things I choose to do. My days are so full of doing for others that I don't do anything for myself. What little time I have I spend exhausted and trying to unwind from the Life Events of the day. Today is my fortieth birthday. I spent the entire day at work, it is nearly eight o'clock in the evening, and I haven't seen my wife. I want to have a better relationship with her, but I don't really know where to start.

E_x = **Egoic Interpretation:** I am not in control of my life anymore. You hear it all the time, how you just wake up one day at eighty years old and realize your whole life has passed you by. At this moment, I feel exactly like that. I have no idea how I got here, but this must be just how my life is.

This example involves applying the Being Equation over a much larger time scale, but we still apply it in the same manner, by looking at what got us to this point and what we need to change. It's important to focus on not getting overwhelmed. Realize that you didn't get to this point overnight, and you will not completely change it overnight, but you can start changing it immediately. Now, write the Being Equation again and work through the variables. It can be helpful to pick a future time frame, for example, one month.

$$B_x(t) = f(SPIL_x E_x)$$

(t) = **Time:** One month from today.

S = **Spirit:** I know I need Spiritual recharge, so I am committing to one backpacking trip and two days of fishing in the next month. I am also going to write in my journal at least five days a week for the next four weeks.

P = **Physical Body:** I know I have treated my Physical Body poorly over the last few years. I am going to commit to at least fifteen minutes of exercise a day for the next thirty days. I need to start slow and be realistic, but I bet I could be jogging a mile or two in thirty days if I start now. I am also going to do twenty push-ups every morning as soon as I wake up.

I = **Inputs:** I need to move. There is so much about this house that does not work for us anymore. Whenever I am in the house, I feel stressed because I know it is too big and too expensive. I am not comfortable in this house anymore. I am going to have a conversation with my wife about moving sometime during the next week.

I also need to change how I eat and cut back substantially on my drinking. I used to eat much healthier when my wife and I cooked meals together at home. Maybe if I ask her about scheduling to cook two meals a week together at home, it would be quality time for us together as well.

L_x = **Life Events:** I don't feel like I control the events that happen in my life anymore. I feel like I am always reacting. A few years ago, I bought a paper calendar and sat down every Sunday evening and scheduled out my upcoming week. I blocked out my exercise time and made sure to schedule a weekly date night with my wife.

My days were still full, but I felt much more in control. I am not sure why I quit doing that, but I am going to buy a paper calendar tomorrow and start doing that again.

I also know that so much of what I do in my life at the moment is dictated by my job, a job that I don't really enjoy anymore. I am going to start thinking about what I would like to do for a job and spend the next thirty days doing some journaling and exercises to see why I ended up in this job and explore what else I might like to do for work.

Most importantly, I am going to schedule some time to have some deep and meaningful conversations with my wife. I am going to schedule a weekend away at a nice hotel so we can get out of our day-to-day environment and reconnect. I want to talk to her about our relationship and see how she is feeling about me. I want to discuss the house and how I feel living here. I want to see if she is happy with how much she works. I know she still cares for me, and I think talking about all of these things in the next thirty days will be a turning point in our marriage. We can make a plan together on how to move forward.

E_x = **Egoic Interpretation:** I got caught up in the Story that you need a big house and a busy job to be *successful*. The idea that the more things you have, the better off you are. I am going to take the next thirty days to start exploring what in my life has led me to think that way. Where does that belief come from? Is it really true that you have to work so hard and sacrifice your relationships and health to be *successful*? I will read and journal about this over the next thirty days.

I hope these two examples of applying the Being Equation have given you some ideas of how to start using the Being Equation in your life. I know the examples are fairly basic, but maybe you see some parallels to your own life. For what it is worth, I didn't just make these up out of thin air. There are definitely parallels to my own life embedded in these examples.

What I would like you to realize is that as you do this process of applying the Being Equation throughout your life, you will begin to change who you are. You will see that every choice you make shapes the Being that you are in the present moment and the Being that you will become. Through this process, you will challenge the underlying stories and even some of your own First Principles on which all of your Egoic Interpretations are built. As you change these, you change who you are.

That all sounds great, you say, but how do I change my life? Change any variable in the Being Equation, and you change your life. Drink a glass of water; your life is changed. Go to the movies; your life is changed. Put away your clean laundry; your life is changed. Get married; your life is changed. Listen to a podcast; your life is changed. Take a breath; your life is changed. Have a thought; your life is changed.

The question is not how to change your life because your life is constantly changing just by you being alive. The question is, how do you consciously choose changes in your life to create the life you want? As I have tried to show, everything that happened to you in the past creates your present, and what you do in the present creates your future. Use the Being Equation to consciously understand your past, so you know who you are in the present moment. You use this knowledge in the present moment to create your future.

This chapter is designed to give you some general examples of applying the Being Equation in your life. The next chapter contains specific exercises you can use to explore each of the five variables of the Being Equation in your own life. The Being Equation is an awareness of what makes you, you. By being conscious of the five variables and applying them in the Being Equation, you can be a conscious creator of your life moving forward.

PART 3

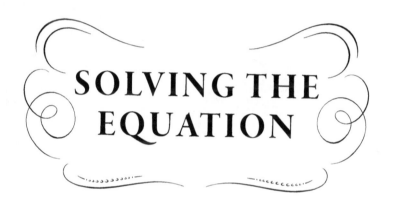

SOLVING THE EQUATION

CHAPTER 15

EXERCISES

Okay, you read most of the book, answered a few *Questions to Consider*, saw two applied examples of the Being Equation, and now you are ready to dig in and explore your own life. All this information is great, but now you may be asking yourself: *how do I start using this in my life?* What follows is a series of exercises you can use to take the information in this book from "book knowledge" to applied knowledge to change your life.

One of the biggest criticisms that exists about books, and content for that matter, is that we have access to so much content and information that we read or see something but forget it in a week or month. If you want this to lodge in your grey matter and change your life, then you need to take action and invest the time it takes.

I assure you, the rewards you reap will far exceed the effort you take in sowing the seeds.

As we have discussed, the true power of the Being Equation comes when we apply it to look at the Being we were in the past and how that created the Being we are in the present moment. We can use this knowledge to create the Being that we want to become in the future. As such, this framework will walk you through each variable of the Being Equation in the context of the past, present, and future.

I would recommend that you begin this exploration by looking at one variable per week. If you decide that you would like to take more than a week with each variable, that is wonderful. However, if you try to do more than a variable per week, you are probably not giving yourself enough time to think about and reflect on each variable and the different exercises. Discovering who you are is not a quick checklist exercise and you are done. As you work through these exercises, give yourself plenty of time and space for reflection. You may not be actively thinking about a question or exercise, but somewhere in the subconscious, your mind is working away on it. You could be out for a walk or doing some grocery shopping, and something will just come to you. Write those things down.

In general, you will use the beginning of the week to look at the past, relevant to the variable of the Being Equation. The middle of the week is used to evaluate the variable in the present, and the end of the week will be focused on what you want for that variable in the future.

At the end of this process, you will be well on your way to seeing and understanding how all that happened in the past shaped who you are in this present moment, and you will have a much clearer idea of who you want to be in the future and how to get there.

Let's be honest. This is a tall order for a single book and a few weeks of your life, but if you put in the effort, the Being Equation will produce the results.

The roots of it all, what I am meant to do, why I make the choices I make, why I feel the way I feel, come back to one question: *who am I?* As we have discussed, on the surface, this sounds like a big, deep, esoteric question. And it is. It is also the question you must be able to answer to address all of the other questions.

It really does then become as simple as cultivating an awareness that the five variables of the Being Equation represent everything that makes you, *you* in this present moment. The practical, applied side of this is, if you want to learn about yourself and grow, then everything you do and everything in your life falls into one of these five categories. These variables are constantly changing, and by knowing what they are, by being aware and curious about them, you can start to shape the direction in which they change.

There are many resources and books and experts in these fields that you can move to from here, but don't let the complexity and depth overwhelm you. It really is as simple as five little variables. When you are feeling overwhelmed, that is likely your mind and ego trying to put the brakes on change and growth. When that happens, the most important thing is not to succumb to confusion. Keep reducing the source of confusion to something simpler and simpler until you get a simple answer.

For example, if you have been struggling for months to decide if the city you live in is the right Input for you, and you have spent the last two hours with lists of pros and cons, and you are more overwhelmed than ever, then simplify until you have an answer. Instead of asking yourself if you need to move to a new city, ask if you need to move to a new house. Ask yourself, *Where do I need to be next month, next week, or tomorrow—or right now?* Maybe you have been sitting at your desk for two hours and need to change your environment to outside at this instant.

Any change in one of these variables changes the Being that you are in the present moment, so let's say you get up and walk outside. It's a beautiful day, the sun is shining, and the trees are covered in spring leaves. You take a deep breath in and exhale and realize that you need more nature in your life. Being outside feels amazing and comforts you. In this moment, you know deep down you need to move no matter what the pro and con lists say. The rest is just the how. The decision is made.

We will dig into specifics for each variable, but this example brings up another general practical application of the Being Equation. If you're feeling "stuck" on something, change one of the five variables. By changing one of the variables, you change the Being that you are. By changing one variable, you may find that the Being that you "were" was stuck. The Being that you are in this present moment doesn't have to be stuck. In the previous example above, a change in Inputs/Environment was all that was needed to go from stuck to clarity. It can be that simple. Sometimes.

As a practice, the first place to start is to always do a quick check-in with each variable in the Being Equation.

This check-in is as simple as:

Spirit, how are you doing? Is there anything you need?

Physical Body, how are you? Is there anything you need?

Inputs—are my environment and the Physical Inputs I am consuming serving me?

Life Events—is there anything on the horizon I need to prepare for?

Ego—where do things stand with you?

It seems silly, but if you do this, you may be surprised by the answers you get back.

There is one more thing we need to revisit before we dive into these exercises, and that is *radical acceptance.* To do this work, you are going to have to radically accept the Being you were in the past and the Being that you are in the present moment. I hope that you will also start to see that you need to radically accept all the Beings in your life for their past actions and who they are in the present moment as well. In Chapter 9, I briefly touched on radical acceptance, but now we need to really take it to heart. Without radical acceptance of yourself and others, it is impossible to go back and objectively look at the Life Events that shaped your life. For the painful ones or the shameful ones, without radical acceptance, it may not even be possible to pull them into consciousness and explore them. If you can't look backward, you can't move forward.

Remember, the person that you were ten years ago, or ten days ago, no longer exists. This same logic also applies to those around you. If you are judging someone today by their actions ten years ago, remember, they are no longer the same person. Regardless of whether you are applying the Being Equation to yourself or to another person, it states that had any Being been born at the exact moment to the same parents and lived through all of the same Life Events up to that very moment, then they would have made the exact same decision. It could have been no other way, so one has to radically accept the action, both when it applies to oneself and to others.

This does not mean you condone the action or wish it weren't different. This only means you accept it, so you can learn, grow, make your choices, and move forward. This is one of those undertakings that falls into the category of simple but not always easy. Radical acceptance is a practice, one you will have to constantly and consciously apply. Refer to the Acceptance and Forgiveness sections of Chapter 9 for a refresher on this topic. Radical acceptance of the self and others is one of the superpowers the Being Equation offers to all of us. Don't underestimate the impact this practice will have on your life. And please don't think of radical acceptance as disempowering. As you will discover by applying it in your life, it is quite the opposite.

Now, it is time for you to get started. What will you need to begin?

- A journal.
- A pen.

Why pen and paper? There is a unique power, almost an alchemy of sorts that comes from writing with a pen on paper. It brings you into the present moment in a way that typing on a computer or phone cannot because both your body and mind are occupied by the process. Not only are you thinking about what to write, but you are bringing in the kinesthetic sense of motion as your hand moves the pen across the page. You hear the pen scratching on the paper and can feel the words being created on the page as you move the pen. Handwriting also causes you to think and create in a more deliberate way. Most of us cannot handwrite as quickly as we can type. It is also much harder to "delete" written words from a piece of paper than to hit the delete key on a computer. For these reasons, we are more focused and think more deliberately when we handwrite.

The act of thinking about each of these exercises and then writing down what comes to mind also provides you with a record you can refer to over time, and it has also been proven that writing by hand aids memory retention and conceptual thinking. The activity of handwriting helps to literally "write" these concepts into your mind. While it is tempting to do this on a computer, tablet, or phone, it is far too easy to be distracted by a notification or to edit your thoughts as you type. Also, be sure to date each page in your journal. I have found it extremely interesting to refer back to previous journal entries months and years later.

Remember, you are using these exercises to explore and learn about the Being that you are. A week per variable is a good pace. If you need more time, take it. Also, be sure not to rush through these exercises. There is no gold star for being the first to finish. The benefit and clarity you receive will be a direct result of the quality of the time and energy you invest.

$$B_x(t) = f(SPIL_xE_x)$$

S = Spirit—Combination of Source Energy and Spiritual Body

If you don't have a relationship with Spirit, then you are missing out on a powerful guiding force of creativity in your life. *We are here for a simple purpose: to create.* To create the lives and experiences we want to have. Think of your Spirit and your Spiritual Body as your partner in helping you identify and create the life and experiences you want to have. Call it intuition, call it whatever you need to so that you will listen to that little inner voice, that feeling, that knowing that comes from deep within. The more you can cultivate that knowing, that relationship, the more powerful and focused you will be. At this point, it doesn't matter what you call it. It only matters that you listen to it. And you also have to nourish it so that it will grow.

SPIRIT EXERCISE ONE

Spend at least ten minutes writing about the origins of and your past experience with your connection to your Spirit.

I have included a few more detailed questions as prompts if you need them:

- What was your past understanding of and relationship to Spirit?
- Where does that understanding of and relationship to Spirit come from?
- Who was the most influential person in your life in conjunction with your relationship with Spirit?
- How old were you when you first became aware of Spirit?
- What are the top three most influential Life Events for you as they relate to Spirit?

Again, I'm playing a broken record here: please do not equate Spirit with religion. It can be useful to use the concept of religion as a point of reference for clarifying your relationship to Spirit, however. If you practice a religion, why? If you don't practice a religion, why? To be clear, I would challenge you to go a few layers deep on any answer that comes up for you. It is not enough to say, "Because my parents practiced a religion" or "Because my parents did not believe in religion."

Tactical Tip: If you are a person who has a hard time journaling on a topic, then here is a great tactic to use:

1. Set a timer for how much time you want to spend writing.
2. Have a rule to keep your pen moving for the entire time.
3. Write whatever comes into your head, no matter what it is. Don't reread or think twice about what you write. If you are supposed to be writing about Spirit, and you think about the stain stick you need to apply to the tomato sauce you spilled on your shirt, write it down. Just keep writing.
4. When the timer goes off, see what you have written, but not before then. If you are still writing, then keep on rolling. The point of the timer is not to tell you when you are done but merely to make sure you get started.

SPIRIT EXERCISE TWO

Spend at least five to ten minutes journaling about how what you discovered in the previous exercise has shaped your relationship with Spirit in the past. Do not move forward from this exercise until you have a clear idea of what your relationship is and how it has been shaped by your past. As the Being Equation shows, Spirit is a major variable in the Beings that we are in the present and the Beings we will become moving forward.

Make sure you can fully answer these questions:

- Do you now understand the origins of your past relationship with Spirit?
- Do you now know who was the most influential person in your life as it relates to your past relationship to Spirit?
- Can you think of any past Life Events that were directly connected to your Spirit or Spiritual Body?

If you can't answer the first two questions or know you phoned in the answers, try again. Remember, you are doing this for you. You deserve your full effort.

SPIRIT EXERCISE THREE

The last two exercises helped you develop an understanding of your past relationship to Spirit. It is now time to look at your relationship in the present moment to Spirit. Has it changed, even just a little, as you have been reading this book? Hopefully, what you have read in this book has impacted how you view Spirit and your Spiritual Body in the present moment.

Take five to ten minutes to journal about your relationship to Spirit and your Spiritual Body in this present moment.

Here are some question prompts:

- Do you believe in the concept of Spirit and a Spiritual Body?
- Did you connect to the idea of a Spiritual Body and a need to nurture it?
- Have you had any experiences in the past that nourished your Spiritual Body?

- Can you think of something you do now that nourishes your Spiritual Body?

Please do physically take the time to put pen to paper and write down your answers. The act of writing will help to clarify your true feelings around Spirit, and there is real power in turning something from thoughts in your head to words on paper.

SPIRIT EXERCISE FOUR

Take a few moments to read back over your journal entry from Spirit exercise three.

Now, take five to ten minutes to journal on the following questions:

- Are you satisfied with your relationship to Spirit as it currently exists, or are there things you would like to change?
- If you are satisfied, why? How has this relationship been serving you?
- If you are not satisfied, why not? What do you need to change?

If you are still struggling with this whole concept of Spirit because you don't believe in god or God, or still equate Spirit with religion, remember, you don't have to believe any of those things to have a relationship with Spirit.

SPIRIT EXERCISE FIVE

Now that you are clear on how your relationship to Spirit was shaped by your past and you understand your current relationship to Spirit and your Spiritual Body, let's figure out what you want this relationship to look like moving forward.

Spend at least ten minutes really thinking about and journaling on what your ideal relationship to Spirit and your Spiritual Body looks like moving forward. For now, don't let the practical considerations of your daily life limit the possibilities of this ideal relationship. For example, if your ideal relationship would take thirty minutes each morning but right now, between taking the dogs out, feeding the kids, and being to work on time, you don't have thirty seconds to spare, don't let that stop you. Design *your ideal relationship without being limited by what is practical.* We will talk about practical later.

Some questions to help:

- If you could wave a magic wand, what would your ideal relationship to Spirit and your Spiritual Body look like moving forward?
- How would you nurture your Spiritual Body?
- What activities would you do to connect with Spirit?
- How often would you do those activities? Would you do something every day? Would you take some time for yourself every month?
- Would you go into nature?
- Would you start a formal practice of some sort?
- What are you going to do on a daily, weekly, and/or monthly basis to connect to the Spirit within you and nurture your Spiritual Body?

This is only the beginning, so I don't want to be too prescriptive on how you do this exercise. You can make a list or write a paragraph or two. It is most important that you come away with what you want your relationship with Spirit to look like for you.

SPIRIT EXERCISE SIX

Now that you have had some time to think about what your ideal relationship with Spirit and your Spiritual Body would look like, let's get practical and tactical. *The goal is that by the end of this exercise, you schedule something to connect with Spirit and nourish your Spiritual Body.*

I would like you to be very practical with what you commit to doing to develop your relationship with Spirit. If this is all new to you, start small. Start with something you know you can commit to and achieve. It could be taking five minutes during the day to read something that nourishes your Spirit. It could be taking five minutes before bed to look at the stars. It could be going for a hike in nature once a week. It doesn't need to be a big thing—it just needs to be *something*. Put it in your calendar and commit to doing it for the next four weeks.

If you already have a Spiritual practice or process by which you connect to Spirit and nurture your Spiritual Body that you enjoy, then view this as a time to refresh and refocus that practice. Or maybe it can be a time to try something new and different, to change it up a bit.

Here are some ideas to try. Read through, and if one or a few resonate with you, then start there:

1. Read poetry.
2. Write poetry.
3. Listen to music.
4. Play music.
5. Meditate.
6. Walk in nature.
7. Pray.
8. Stand outside barefoot.
9. Light a candle and watch the flame.

10. Build a campfire.
11. Do yoga.
12. Visit a holy place—you don't have to be a practitioner of a religion to visit a holy site.
13. Read a daily inspirational tidbit from a Spiritual path—it could be Buddhist, Islamic, Hindu, Christian, Druid, Native American, you name it—any of the true Spiritual teachings can resonate regardless of their origins.
14. Journal—I connect with my Spirit when I journal.
15. Create Pottery.
16. Go for a walk in a graveyard—I know, it sounds creepy, but a graveyard during the day can be a Spiritual reminder that the body we inhabit is only temporary, and this realization can help us connect more deeply with our Spiritual Body.
17. Draw.
18. Paint.

The point here is that your Spiritual practice can be anything that creates a connection between you and your Spirit. This connection will nourish your Spirit and the health of your Spiritual Body, and the connection will grow. It is important to understand that this is not a one-time thing. It is a Spiritual *practice*, and practice means you do it on a regular basis. I am not saying that you need to do it every day, but the more you can connect with and nourish your Spirit and Spiritual Body, the better. If you listen, your Spirit will tell you what it needs.

$$B_x(t) = f(SPIL_xE_x)$$

P = Physical Body—Genetics and Epigenetics of Being

Most of us learned that our Physical Body, through our genetics and DNA, was set at birth. I hope that Chapter 4 cracked the door open for you to believe that this may not be entirely the case. At a minimum, we know we can switch certain genes on and off using epigenetic changes to our DNA. As I write these words in the year 2020, I anticipate what we know will be drastically expanded in ten or twenty years.

From a practical standpoint, let's think about genetics and epigenetics as the driving forces that shape our Physical Body and the baseline for how we have been programmed to react to the information coming in through our five physical senses. I want you to stop thinking of your genetics as a single set point but instead as a spectrum of possibility. Your genetics establish the absolute boundaries of what is physically possible, but there are many things that are within your control that determine where you fall within this range of possibility. For example, do you think your exact height is determined at birth, or do you think the foods you eat, your nutritional status while you are growing and developing, play a role in how tall you will ultimately be? Do you think your vision quality is set at birth, or do you think staring at a computer screen for thirty years for twelve hours a day impacts the quality of your eyesight?

PHYSICAL BODY EXERCISE ONE

Take ten minutes to journal about the beliefs that you have received from your family or anyone in your life that has shaped how you see yourself physically showing up in the world. Take time to think about how you see your biological parents in terms of how your perception of their Physical Bodies has shaped who you are.

Do you think you will end up looking like your mother/father when you reach their age? Have you ever consciously thought about whether you hold this belief? If they have health issues, do you hold the belief that those same health issues are destined to happen to you? Is there a true genetic reason that you should be preparing for a future physical health concern?

There is a fine line between being aware of and preparing for a future possibility and focusing so much on a future possibility that you turn it into reality. It is important to become aware of which side of the line you are standing on.

Were there specific Life Events that you remember that have defined your physical self-image? Look for phrases like:

- "You are built just like your father/mother."
- "Everyone in our family is _____."
- "Your whole family is built just like _____."
- "Nobody in our family is good at _____."
- "Everyone in our family is good at _____."
- "When it comes to _____, your sister/brother got all the talent."
- "Everyone in our family suffers from (insert an illness/disease here)."
- "We have longevity in our genes."

The truth is most of us have a negative self-image when it comes to our physical appearance or physical abilities. Did these questions bring up negative experiences for you? The opposite can also be true. You could have positive views around these questions. If you do, that is fantastic. In either case, take these ten minutes to reflect on the

Life Events that have shaped how you see your physical self showing up in the world and how that appearance could shape your future.

Tactical Tip: What you write in this exercise is only for you. Sometimes, it is difficult to write down things that we feel are a negative reflection on those around us. You need to write down the truth—your truth—and how these beliefs have shaped you.

PHYSICAL BODY EXERCISE TWO

As you saw in Chapter 4, epigenetics play a strong role in the Being that you are. If possible, start a conversation with your relatives about what they know about your ancestors. Some families may have talked extensively about their history, but most have not. Get curious about relatives who you have never met or may have passed before you were born. Find out where they lived, what their lives were like, what they lived through. Major world-historical events can shape epigenetics. If your grandparents or great grandparents lived through a world war, a famine, a great depression, or a holocaust, then chances are these events somehow shaped your epigenetics.

Take ten minutes to journal about what you have learned through this process.

- Were there any big surprises for you?
- Did you learn any family history that could be linked to epigenetics?

PHYSICAL BODY EXERCISE THREE

In this exercise, let's focus on the Physical Body. As you have seen, whether you have been conscious of it or not, your Life Events and the Egoic Interpretations of those Life Events have shaped what you believe is possible for you physically. I want you to think of your genetics and epigenetics as a spectrum of potential, from low to high, bad to good, however you need to approach it instead of a fixed set point.

With this in mind, journal about the following in relation to your Physical Body and your five senses:

- What is my relationship to my Physical Body in this present moment?
- Do I like my Physical Body?
- Do I take care of my Physical Body? How?
- Do I accept that I am in control of my body and appearance, or do I believe I am a victim of my genes?
- Am I realizing my "highest and best" genetic potential, however I define highest and best? (While there is no judgment in this question as to what "highest and best" means, you need to be honest with yourself about what it means to you.)
- Do I view my Physical Body as an asset or a liability? Why?

Tactical Tip: This topic can be triggering for many of us because of what society would have us believe about our bodies and body image. Be gentle but honest with yourself about what your thoughts and beliefs are around your Physical Body in this moment. If you are happy with your Physical Body, wonderful, write down all the reasons why. If you are unhappy, write down all the reasons why. If you have been pretending to yourself or others that you are happy or unhappy, this is the time to be honest. Tell the truth to yourself and write it down. Be real about where you are in this present moment. Remember, you must know where you are starting if you want to know where you are going.

I would be remiss not to talk about body image when discussing this section, as so many of us look at our parents and grandparents and automatically see what we think we will become. Personally, I heard a thousand times growing up, "You're built just like your father." We become programmed that we are destined to have the same body shape as our parents. If they are "healthy" this can be a good thing. If they are "not healthy" this lays a dangerous foundation. Going down the rabbit hole of defining "healthy" and "not healthy" is not beneficial here. You will decide what that means to you, but I do want to break the notion that we are strongly predisposed to have a body type like our parents as we age.

Some things are genetically out of your control, like your hair or eye color, for instance. However, do not let the insidious little thought lurk in the back of your mind that if your parents or grandparents or brothers and sisters, for that matter, started carrying extra pounds as they aged, that you are destined to do the same. This is just not the case, but we let this type of thinking creep in, not only with our weight but with so many aspects of ourselves. For example, with beliefs like: the men in our family have heart attacks young, we don't have great longevity genes in our family, or diabetes runs in our family. Well, maybe that is because the past four generations of the family have smoked, drank, ate an unhealthy diet, and were severely overweight. That is not genetic. That is the result of poor choices and habits—many of them made repeatedly. For most of your characteristics, your genes create the range of values that is possible. It is up to you to determine where you land within that range of values. For many of these traits, your daily choices matter. Habits can change.

Remember, your Physical Body is your connection to the physical world. Your body is how you move through and interact with this world. Your five senses control your physical experience in this world. Your physical experience shapes your entire experience.

PHYSICAL BODY EXERCISE FOUR

Throughout this section, my goal has been to reinforce with you that the potential of your Physical Body as it relates to genetics and epigenetics is not a set point but a spectrum of possibility. It is now time for you to decide where on your spectrum of possibility you would like to be in the future. Think of this category as anything that relates to your Physical Body or one of your five physical senses. Most people immediately jump to body size or physical condition, but let's talk about the sense of smell to expand your thinking.

Most people don't think too much about their sense of smell or how to develop it further, but let's imagine your goal was to improve your sense of smell. It is a physical sense, so why not? Most people would think that you were born with a sense of smell, and you get what you get, but is that really the case? I would argue that you have a spectrum of ability to your sense of smell, and just as you may never be the fastest sprinter in the world, chances are you can be a faster sprinter than you are now. The same possibilities apply to smell. You may never be the best "smeller" in the world, but you can be much better than you are now. How? By training your nose. By taking a class on perfume making or wine tasting. Anything that trains and refines your sense of smell. Go outside and smell all the flowers that are blooming in your yard or at the botanical gardens. Smell each bottle of hand soap or lotion at the grocery store. Stop and smell your food before you eat it. Train your nose, and before you know it, you will be picking up scents where before you were just breathing air. A whole new world will open to you.

You can do this with all of your senses. Go outside and see how many distinct shades of green you can identify in your yard. How many shades of yellow or orange can you see in the sunset?

Here is another fun exercise related to physical touch. Pick a spot and sit outside either as the sun rises or as the sun sets. Expose some skin and concentrate on trying to feel the change in air temperature. Try to notice the exact moment when you feel a temperature change, hotter or cooler. See how many temperature changes you can feel in fifteen minutes. This can be even more dramatic if you can sit in a spot that moves from full sun to shade or vice versa over that time frame.

Here is your task: Over the next twenty-four hours, pick one of your five senses and start a training program. Explore the sense, get to know it a bit, push your limits, and journal about your experience. Try one of the activities I've suggested. Realize that there are many more physical changes you can make other than your physical appearance.

PHYSICAL BODY EXERCISE FIVE

For this exercise, explore something that has come up for you related to your Physical Body, genetics, or epigenetics. It could be anything from the week's exercises that surprised you that you want to revisit. It could be a place where you have some curiosity and would like to explore more. And you also have one more task. In the next twenty-four hours, do something that nurtures your Physical Body. It can be anything you choose. The only requirement is that it nurtures and supports your Physical Body.

Here are ten ideas to get you started:

1. Do some light stretching or yoga.
2. Go for a walk.
3. Go in a sauna.
4. Drink twenty ounces of water.
5. Have a cup of green tea.

6. Eat an apple.
7. Focus on your breathing for five minutes.
8. Give yourself a manicure or pedicure.
9. Take a hot bath.
10. Take an ice bath.

You can pick from this list or do anything of your choosing, but do something. After you have done something for your Physical Body, take ten minutes to journal about the experience. Did you choose something you do on a regular basis or something new? How did it make your body feel?

Bonus Activity: Order a genetic test kit from one of the gene sequencing companies and see what you can find out about your genetics (this is being written in 2020). Fair warning, I have friends who found new family members or learned things about their family history that they had never known. It can be quite an adventure!

$$B_x(t) = f(SPIL_xE_x)$$

I = Inputs—Physical and Environmental Inputs of Being

Inputs is the easiest of the five variables of the Being Equation to change from moment to moment. If you do not like where you are sitting, get up and move. If you don't like the food or drink you are putting in your body, stop eating or drinking it. We can literally change the Being that we are in any given instant by changing this variable.

Remember that every Being or object in your environment emits energy and has a vibration relative to you. You need to become aware of this vibration and decide if the vibration is serving you. The key is to regularly examine the Beings and objects in your environment. If you are trying to accomplish a specific task or objective, you need to consciously create your Inputs and environment to facilitate that objective. If an object or Being is no longer supporting you, then you have to be willing to let go of that object or Being. *You need to get in the habit of consciously curating your environment and Inputs to facilitate who you want to be.*

For example, if you were beginning to meditate, you would not go to the middle of Grand Central Station in New York at rush hour for your first meditation session. You would choose a quiet, calming environment that minimizes distractions to give you the greatest likelihood of success.

If you were trying to eat a healthy meal, you would likely not choose to go to Bill's Big House of Burgers and Beers. Instead, a restaurant specializing in healthy, whole-food meals would be a better choice.

Of course, these are extreme examples. We make small choices that have this kind of effect on who we are each day. They may not be as obvious, but they are still there. When you are at the store, you decide whether to buy a six-pack of seltzer water or a six-pack of soda, not a big decision. However, that decision determines later that evening whether you will have a soda with dinner or a seltzer. After work, you decide whether to go to happy hour with Joe or meet Chris for racquetball. You decide whether to keep that stack of six books on your desk that you haven't read in a year and that makes you feel bad every time you look at them, or that it is time to donate them to the local library. You decide whether to add an orchid to your kitchen window to bring some color and life to the space or to keep it stark sterile. These choices are up to you, but each one of these choices affects the Being that you are in the moment and the Being that you will become.

This is a very exciting week because you will use these exercises to see exactly how quickly changing the Inputs in your life can change your life. As the examples discussed in Chapter 5 show, changing the Inputs in the Being Equation can immediately, and drastically, change the Being that you are.

INPUTS EXERCISE ONE

Think about the environment of your childhood. This is a very big topic, and, in reality, it will not be possible for you to explore and cover all of the ground for this variable in a day, or a week for that matter, so view this exercise as a starting point. With that said, let's get started.

Take at least ten minutes (or maybe even much longer) to journal about the environment of your childhood. Think of your childhood as the years from your earliest memories through your teenage years. For this exercise, let's focus on your childhood home and neighborhood.

Describe the home:

- Was it a house, an apartment, or a portion of a house?
- Was it in the city or in the country?
- How many people lived in the area?
- Was it in a small town or thriving metropolis?
- How many family members lived with you?
- Was it a fairly quiet home or was it always buzzing with activity?

When you think back on the space and the place, what is one word you would use to describe the overall feeling of this childhood space? Why did you choose that word? If you are having difficulty, this exercise can benefit greatly from using the timer strategy described in an earlier tactical tip. The more you immerse yourself in this exercise, the more valuable it will be moving forward.

Tactical Tip: If you lived in more than one home during your childhood, do this exercise for each place. Compare and contrast the feeling and your memories from each of your childhood homes.

INPUTS EXERCISE TWO

This exercise will focus on remembering the Physical Inputs of your childhood. Everything that you have consumed—sights, sounds, smells, foods, drugs, you name it, up to this very moment have made you the Being you are.

Take ten minutes to think about the Physical Inputs of your childhood:

- What were the five most common dinner meals served in your home?
- What was your favorite breakfast?
- Were you allowed fast food and candy, or was it granola and vegetables? TV dinners or meals made from scratch?
- Was the television always on, or was it one hour a day?
- Was there "quiet time" or was it always "chaos time"?
- Would you say the Physical Inputs of your childhood were generally healthy or unhealthy? Why?

The point of this exercise is for you to take this time to really get a sense of the Physical Inputs that literally shaped the Being that you are today.

INPUTS EXERCISE THREE

Journal for ten minutes about your current home, including the geographic location, and how it makes you feel:

- What does the space look like?
- How long have you lived there?
- Why do you live there?
- What do you like most about the space?
- What do you like least about the space?
- How do you like the geographic location?
- When you have been away from your home, are you happy to return?
- Is your home too big, too small, or just right?
- If you were going to live there another five years, what are three things you would do to change or improve the home?
- If you share your home with others, do you have a little space that is only yours?
- What is your favorite object in your home?

- What is your least favorite object in your home?
- In a single word, how does your current home make you feel?
- Why did you choose that word?

By the end of this exercise, you should be starting to get an overall sense of how your home and its geographic location are affecting the Being that you are.

INPUTS EXERCISE FOUR

Now, it is time to focus on your Physical Inputs. Your Physical Body is how you interact with the physical world. Without it, you could experience nothing about the physical world. Take a minute to think about the role of your Physical Body in your life. It is only through your five senses that you have any interaction with the physical world. Without your body, you would not feel the touch of a lover, see the smile of a child, hear the laughter of your friends, taste a perfectly ripe tomato straight from the vine, or smell the scent of jasmine on the air of a summer evening. Your body is your vessel for moving through this world. How do you treat it?

Take ten minutes, or perhaps longer, to write a letter to your Physical Body. Write this letter as if you were writing a letter to a friend, because your body is your friend. Thank your body for everything it has done for you up to this point. Write about your current habits, the things that you consume, and tell your body why you consume things. Ask your body how it feels about the things you consume and if they are serving the needs of your body, and listen to the answer. Write down what your body says back to you in the letter.

Tactical Tip: For some of you, writing a letter to your body will seem strange. Most of us have opinions on what we should consume or what our body's needs are based on what we have learned from others. This exercise is designed for you to listen to your body and see if it tells you what it needs and what you consume that is serving it and you, or not serving. The hard part about this exercise is that we often don't like or want to hear the answers we hear back from our body.

INPUTS EXERCISE FIVE

It is time to start designing the environment that will best support the Being you want to become. Everything in your environment creates the Being that you are. In exercise three of this section, you looked at how your present environment is affecting you. What about your present environment needs to change? Now is the time to start making those changes. Some of them will be small changes like getting rid of that couch you have had since college or buying a new house plant. Others may be much larger, for example, realizing your current home is not serving you at all, and it is time to move. No matter the changes you need to make, do not feel overwhelmed. Feel grateful that now you know what you need to do. The rest is only a matter of time.

In your journal, make a numbered list from one to eleven down the left-hand side of the page, then take a few minutes and read back over your journal entry from exercise three. As you read, next to each number, write down every item that comes up that you can change to enhance your living environment. It doesn't only have to be things you need to remove from your environment. It could be things that you really like that you want to display more prominently. For example, my wife and I purchased a pottery heart in Mexico that we had not hung on the wall after we moved. I found it in a box and immediately hung it on the wall, and we both enjoy seeing it each day. Write down each item that comes up no matter how large or small, from buying another house plant to moving to a new country. If you need more than eleven lines, then add more to your list, but you must have at least eleven items. Now go do one of those eleven items right now. The exercise is complete when you have done at least one item.

INPUTS EXERCISE SIX

Now that you have had some time and space to reflect on the letter that you wrote to your body, what is coming up for you? Are you happy with the Inputs you're using to fuel your Physical Body? Are they serving you? You need to approach this exercise with zero judgment. Learn from the past, but do not beat yourself up about your decisions of the past. You were a different person then.

Today, your mission is to design a simple framework for the Inputs you want for your body moving forward. The result of this does not need to be a super prescriptive diet plan, but instead, think of it as creating your First Principles for the Inputs that you want to use to fuel your body. These can be things you want to stop doing, as well as things you want to start doing. For example, in your letter, your body may have told you that it doesn't feel good after you drink soda. You may decide you no longer want to drink soda. Or maybe you decide that every meal needs to include at least one serving of fruit or vegetables. The goal is to come up with a simple list of guiding principles for how you want to fuel your body. If you spend the time now to think about it and come up with these principles, then you will not have to think about it every time you have to make a decision. Think about it this time, so you don't have to think about it every time.

Here is a list of examples, but please create your own:

- I do not drink soda.

- I do drink at least five glasses of water per day.
- I do not eat candy bars.
- I do eat as much fruit as I want.
- My plate is mostly vegetables and/or fruit.
- I do not eat fast food.
- I do not drink caffeine after three o'clock in the afternoon so I can sleep better.
- I have a "two alcoholic drink-a-day" limit.

Tactical Tip: As you write these guiding principles, realize that these are the ideal. Some may be negotiable, but others are not. In reality, you may not meet these guiding principles all of the time. I certainly do not meet all of mine, but at least I am conscious of not meeting them each time it happens. It is going to happen, and that is okay. For example, as a guiding principle, I do not drink soda, but a few times a year, I have a Dr. Pepper because it is nostalgic from my childhood and a rare, special treat. This is a conscious decision; I enjoy it, then carry on with my better daily habits of drinking water and seltzer in place of the multiple daily sodas I drank as a kid. Being conscious about these decisions means I have the opportunity to decide if I need to consider a change to my choices or enjoy the splurge and the experience that comes with it.

There is a great saying in meditation. When you get distracted and lost in thought, simply begin again. The same is true for these guiding principles. If you get off track and have that candy bar, simply begin again.

INPUTS EXERCISE SEVEN

The previous exercises have focused on your physical environment and Physical Inputs you consume. There has been very little direct focus on some of the other Inputs in your life that are not as obvious, specifically technological. Phones, computers, televisions, email, text, Facebook, Twitter, and many more yet to come. Content is being created constantly, and you are consuming it. The content that was consumed in the days of old, including print periodicals, hard copy books, and print newspapers, was all physical. You could set them down and walk away. There was a distinct beginning, middle, and end. When you finished reading a paper, you couldn't immediately "click" on another paper and start reading it.

During my freshman year of college, I gained fifty pounds. I grew up in a household and a community in which cleaning your plate at each meal was taught and considered an important sign of respect. You were given a portion of food, you ate it all, and then, you could ask for more if you wanted it. I like food, so I often had seconds. The trouble for me came that when I went to college, there was a place called the dining hall, D-Hall for short, for every meal. At D-Hall, there were many different dining options, and you could take as much food as you liked. I could eat all different types of foods at every meal. I couldn't stop trying one more thing or having just a few more bites. The result was I overconsumed at every meal, three times a day.

The same issues can appear when it comes to digital content in this day and age, but it is actually slightly worse than an unlimited buffet of content. Instead of having to go to the dining hall three times a day, we carry the dining hall in our pockets. We never leave the buffet. We keep on consuming.

Digital content and its availability are fairly new phenomena for us humans.

Take ten minutes today to journal about your consumption of digital content:

- Are you consuming it wisely, or have you put on a few digital pounds yourself?
- What would a healthy relationship with digital content look like to you?
- Is your content consumption healthy now?
- Would it be one big dose of content, one time a day, or would you break it into a few smaller portions throughout the day?
- Can you stay focused on the content you're searching for, or do you easily get distracted?
- Are you in control of the content you consume, or is the content consuming you?

Use this awareness to start thinking about your digital consumption. Similar to your list of guiding principles for Physical Inputs, come up with a list of guiding principles for digital Inputs. Be honest and realistic, but have at least three guiding principles before you complete this exercise.

$$B_x(t) = f(SPIL_xE_x)$$

L_x = Life Events

Since a Life Event can be thought of as anything that happened to you and left a memory, conscious and/or subconscious, everything that has ever happened to you is a Life Event. By definition, this becomes a nearly impossible topic to cover with a few exercises. Before we start, realize that this is only the beginning. As you continue to use the Being Equation, Life Events from your past that you thought were completely insignificant will rear their heads up and show you they were actually quite profound. Remember that third-grade art teacher that said you were not very good at art, or the girl who dumped you in seventh grade, or that one time that Mom thought Dad was picking you up from school and Dad thought Mom was picking you up from school and neither picked you up? All of these Life Events are still there, and as you start poking around, I am sure you will find a few surprises.

LIFE EVENTS EXERCISE ONE

I originally learned a version of this exercise from a mentor, Philip McKernan, and it can be extremely powerful.

Take ten minutes (or more) to journal about the five most positive Life Events that you have had in your life up to this point. Do this by creating a list of one through five in your journal, listing each event, and writing one sentence to describe the Life Event. Now, below the list, write a paragraph or so on each of these Life Events and what specifically made you feel special.

These Life Events do not have to be the typical "best" Life Events that we traditionally think of, like the day you got married or the birth of your children. These should be the five Life Events that made you feel the absolute best you have ever felt. It could be winning the fifty-yard dash in first grade, a day spent fishing with your father, your first bike ride without training wheels, a promotion at work, or the day the fire truck came to your birthday party (that happened to me but only because our chimney was on fire).

As you review your list of Life Events and the paragraph about each, answer these questions:

- Do you see any commonalities in the Life Events?
- Did most involve a certain type of setting (i.e., inside, outside, someplace specific)?
- Were most around a certain type of activity?
- Did most involve being around other people, or were they more solitary pursuits?

Take a minute or two to write down these commonalities.

LIFE EVENTS EXERCISE TWO

You knew this was coming, didn't you? Take ten minutes (or more) to journal about your five most negative Life Events. Do this by creating a list of one to five in your journal, listing each event, and writing one sentence to describe the Life Event. Now, below the list, write a paragraph or so on each of these Life Events and what specifically made you feel so negatively.

A word of caution: if any of these focus on a specific type of trauma involving abuse of any sort or other major triggering events, it may be best to not do this exercise. This can bring up feelings and emotions that are best treated with professional guidance from a licensed mental health professional. If you think some counseling would be beneficial, I highly recommend you seek it.

These Life Events do not have to be the typical "worst" Life Events that we traditionally think of, like the day you got divorced or the death of a parent. These should be the five Life Events that made you feel the absolute worst you have ever felt. One could be being the last person in your entire first-grade class to finish the fifty-yard dash, a day spent fishing with your father (it was cold, raining, and you hate fishing), when you went to the hospital after wrecking your bike during your first ride without training wheels, a demotion at work, or the day the fire truck came to your birthday party because your chimney was on fire.

I am making light here because this is a tough topic. Be prepared to be gentle with yourself. It can bring up some very difficult feelings and emotions.

As you review your list of Life Events and the paragraph about each, answer these questions:

- Do you see any commonalities in the Life Events?
- Did most involve a certain type of setting?
- Were most around a certain type of event or activity?
- Did most involve being around other people, or were they more solitary?

Take a minute or two to write down these commonalities.

Now, go do something fun and lighthearted. Switch up your energy. That was a tough exercise.

LIFE EVENTS EXERCISE THREE

Let's take a look at the Life Events of your present reality. Take out your calendar and think back over the last two days of your life. For this exercise, they should be the last two "typical" days. If you are in Fiji on vacation, those don't count, unless you are typically in Fiji on vacation, and then they count.

Make a numbered list of one to five and write down the five best things that happened to you during those two days. They could be things like a great workout, your dog snuggling with you in bed, a great cup of coffee, or an excellent meditation. Whatever they are, make a list.

Now, look at those same two days and identify the five worst things that happened with a numbered list. You know the drill for how to do this.

Now, was it harder for you to make a list of the five best things or the five worst things? If it was harder to make a "best" list, why? If it was harder to make a "worst" list, why?

If your "best" list was overflowing, congratulations! If your "worst" list was overflowing, let's use the next few exercises to see how to change that by adding in some new Life Events into your world.

LIFE EVENTS EXERCISE FOUR

This is a multi-part exercise. Do not read forward to the next portion until you complete the portion you are working on. Seriously, no peeking.

PART ONE

I want you to close your eyes (after reading the rest of this paragraph) for five minutes and imagine that you are living a life in which the people around you, the ones who are most important to you, support you unconditionally in the decisions you make regarding who and what you want to be. If you want pink hair, have pink hair. If you decide to never wear a suit and tie again, great. If you want take a year off to write poetry, take the year off. If you decide to get your body covered in tattoos, ink up! Want to cut your hair short, grow your hair long, shave your hair off, join the circus, study ancient Chinese literature, sail around the world, ride a motorcycle, or hike the Appalachian Trail? Go for it! What would you be or do if there were no judgment, only support from the most important people in your life?

Journal for ten minutes on what this imagined life would look like. Set the timer and keep the pen moving. Write all about it, stream-of-consciousness style. Describe whatever comes to mind for you. Don't think, just write.

PART TWO

When I asked the question in part one, who was the first person that came to your mind as having the biggest impact based on their approval or judgment of your decisions?

PART THREE

Are they worthy of having this influence? Do you want them to have this control through judgment over your life and the Life Events you choose to create? Why or why not? To be clear, if the judgment of another controls the decisions you make in your life, they do have a level of control over you. I am not saying this is positive or negative, but it is certainly something you should be aware of moving forward.

LIFE EVENTS EXERCISE FIVE

It is time to start looking to the future, so in this exercise, you will write your eulogy. It seems rather morbid to sit down and write your own eulogy, but in this exercise, I would like you to turn that notion on its head.

PART ONE

I want you to write a eulogy, not for the person you are now, but for the person that you want to be at the end of your life. Will you have been a world traveler, a poet, a parent, a circus clown, a CEO, a coach, an Appalachian Trail thru-hiker, a blue-ribbon winner for pie baking at the state fair, a chess master, a quilter, a bike racer? There are so many possibilities. Think of everything you hope to accomplish and put it in there *with this caveat: I only want you to include what you want to be for yourself, not what you think you need to be for others.*

PART TWO

Now, look at all the cool things you will have done by the end of your life. What do you have to start doing or being right now to become that person? Get after it!

A big step to creating who you want to be is to proactively create the Life Events that will help you become the Being you want to become. Getting out in nature is a Life Event. Attending a workshop is a Life Event. Having a conversation with a potential mentor is a Life Event. Leaving a job you despise is a Life Event. Don't wait for these things to fall into your lap. Go create them.

LIFE EVENTS EXERCISE SIX

In the previous two exercises, you got a glimpse of the Being you want to be in the future and have an indication of what might be holding you back. It is time to take this knowledge and get tactical about what Life Events you need to create in the present to create the Being you want to be in the future. For this exercise, take ten minutes to think about and answer the following question: what kind of Life Events would be happening to the Being I am right now to create the Being I want to be in the future? You can make a list of Life Events or write it in paragraph form. The purpose is for you to start to get a list of the Life Events that need to happen for you to become the Being you want to be. In reality, this is a big exercise, and ten minutes will only be scratching the surface. Take as much time and space as you need to answer this. Realize that this is simply a start and is a useful exercise to revisit on a regular basis.

Tactical Tip: I personally use this exercise at the start of each day or when I don't know what to do next. I simply ask myself: *what Life Events would be happening right now to the Being I want to create in the future?* The answer is: *whatever I make happen.*

If the person you want to be is a writer, chances are that person would pick up a pen and write something every day. If the person you want to be is clean and organized, chances are a Life Event for them would be to clean and straighten their kitchen every day. If the person you want to be is Spiritually-connected to their Source, chances are they have a Spiritual practice that is a Life Event for them each day.

The key is that you have to answer this question without letting your old friend ego jump in and start creating judgment or a Story around the Life Events you want to create. Often, ego likes to challenge us or strives to maintain the status quo. Our ego doesn't always like change, so if you are consciously creating Life Events that will change you from the Being you are now to the Being you want to be in the future, then your ego may be feeling threatened and will try to keep you from doing these things. Recognize that, thank your ego, and move on. Go create the Life Events that will move you towards who you want to be.

And one more thing. This is no place for fear. Fear will come up when you do new things. It always does. It doesn't matter how big or how small the Life Event appears. Our ego and mind will try to use fear as a tool to keep us from doing something that could change the status quo. Do not, I repeat, do not let fear hold you back on this one. Go ahead and imagine the possibilities as if fear was no limitation. If you hear a little voice ask, *Who do you think you are to...?* Or maybe it says, *You could never...* that is ego talking. Along those lines, if you have a friend or family member say something similar to you, recognize that is their fear talking. It means you are on the right track. Thank them, then look forward, spread your wings, and take the leap! Fly you precious Being, fly!

$$B_x(t) = f(SPIL_xE_x)$$

E_x = Egoic Interpretation of Life Event

Your Egoic Interpretations of Life Events are ultimately controlled in the moment by your ego. The title of a book by Ryan Holiday sums up the popular belief regarding ego, and that title, *Ego is the Enemy*,[8] is one way to approach your ego. You can view it as something you have to constantly see as an adversary, something to always be cautiously mindful of; this is a very practical approach. As the concept of ego has been used throughout history, there are many fine examples of people whose ego got the better of them.

Although the word "ego" comes from psychology, the idea of dissolution of ego, or self, is a central objective of Buddhism. Why? Because the ego can make us do silly and dangerous things, so it's best to get rid of it. However, as many people throughout history have also realized, this is not an easy thing to do, and if one gets serious about this quest to dissolve ego, it can lead to living in monasteries, long periods of isolation, and the need to give away all one's worldly possessions. I am not making light of the practice of getting rid of ego. On the contrary, it seems like a worthy goal to attempt to attain, but let's approach this from a practical standpoint. What can you do in the here and now to influence your ego, and therefore, your Egoic Interpretation of Life Events as they occur? This is important because your ego helps determine each and every Egoic Interpretation not only as it occurs but also as you assign new Egoic Interpretations to Life Events that have already occurred.

Be aware you have an ego.

---

8   R. Holiday, Ego is the Enemy: The Fight to Master Our Greatest Opponent (Portfolio, 2016).

By definition, the Being Equation implies that every Being has an ego because, without it, there would be no Egoic Interpretation of a Life Event, and every Life Event *does* have an Egoic Interpretation. With this knowledge, realize that we all have an ego, which does not necessarily have to be a bad thing. Make friends with your ego. Get to know it. As with many things, awareness is the first step.

Have conversations with your ego:

- Do I need that Ferrari to feel good, or is that my ego talking?
- Do I need those nine-hundred-dollar shoes to feel good, or is that my ego talking?
- Do I need to put on makeup and style my hair for yoga class, or is that my ego talking?

EGOIC INTERPRETATION EXERCISE ONE

Throughout this book, you have been learning about your ego and how it creates your Egoic Interpretation. Make a list. Write one through five down on the left of your journal page and write five times where, for lack of a better term, your ego got the best of you. These can be big things or small things. Remember the laundry example from Chapter 7.

- Are there any Life Events that are recurring for you that create negative Egoic Interpretations?
- Was there one big Life Event that makes you cringe each time you crack the crate open and look at that Egoic Interpretation?

Write it down.

Take some time and write a paragraph about each event. What commonalities exist between the five events you have listed?

EGOIC INTERPRETATION EXERCISE TWO

Now, let's do the same thing for when your ego was at its best. Write one through five down the left side of your journal page and write five times where you were on the positive side of Egoic Interpretation. These can be big things or small things. Remember the laundry example from Chapter 7.

- Are there any Life Events that are recurring for you that create positive Egoic Interpretations?
- Was there one big Life Event that makes you really feel good each time you crack the crate open and look at that Egoic Interpretation?

Write it down.

Take some time and write a paragraph about each event. Do you see any commonality between the five events you have listed?

As has been discussed, you do have a powerful tool in your relationship to ego. *You know four other variables you can use to influence ego and Egoic Interpretation.* This is not theoretical. Every variable in the Being Equation influences every other in any situation. You can maximize the other four variables in the Being Equation to influence your ego and Egoic Interpretation at any given moment. If you are doing a great job of taking care of your Spiritual Body, that will change who you are as a Being, and chances are your Being will have a positive influence on your ego and Egoic Interpretation. If you're hungry and hungover, your ego is going to react very differently to the half-and-half container being empty at the coffee shop than if you are well-rested and feeling healthy. Your ego and Egoic Interpretation do not occur in isolation.

EGOIC INTERPRETATION EXERCISE THREE

For one of the items on your list in exercise one, write out the condition of the other four variables in the Being Equation for when that Egoic Interpretation event occurred. Do this in the same style as the two examples from Chapter 14. Write down the variable and then write a paragraph about the status of the variable during the Life Event that created the Egoic Interpretation.

- What was the status of your Spirit?
- What was the condition of your Physical Body?
- What was the physical environment like?

Dig in and get curious about all of these variables and start to see how they influenced your Egoic Interpretation in that moment.

EGOIC INTERPRETATION EXERCISE FOUR

Now choose an item from your list when your ego was at its best and do the same process as in exercise three. Write out the condition of the other four variables in the Being Equation for when that Egoic Interpretation event occurred. Write down the variable and then write a paragraph about the status of the variable during the Life Event that created the Egoic Interpretation. What was the status of your Spirit? What was the condition of your Physical Body? What were the Inputs (Physical and Environmental) like? Dig in and get curious about all of these things and start to see how they influenced your Egoic Interpretation in that moment.

I hope that working through exercises three and four gave you practice with applying the Being Equation to your own life and that you can see how easy it can be to do. Besides the knowledge that you can use the other four variables in the Being Equation to influence Egoic Interpretation, one of the most powerful things you can do in the present moment to affect Egoic Interpretation is to be conscious of the Egoic Interpretation you are assigning before filing a Life Event away.

Check your Egoic Interpretation before you file the Life Event away.

Once you file it away, your Egoic Interpretation is going to stick with that Life Event until you bring it back into consciousness. Before you close the lid on it, do a quick check and be sure that is the Egoic Interpretation you want the Life Event to have.

For example, maybe you think back over the Life Event that just occurred and realize:

- That was a really nice dinner with my wife. I was just stressed from work, and that made me not enjoy it.
- Even though I couldn't focus, that was a great meditation.
- Although only three people read the article I wrote, I learned a lot while writing it, and I had fun.

Doing this quick check-in gives you the opportunity to change that Story before filing it away.

EGOIC INTERPRETATION EXERCISE FIVE

Can you think of a Life Event that happened in the last twenty-four hours (I know it is not the exact present moment) that you can assign a new Egoic Interpretation to before you file it deep within the storehouse of your grey matter? I bet you can. Write about it in your journal.

Here it is, the final exercise of this chapter. I believe if you can start to implement this tool in your life, you will be amazed at what will happen. Remember in Chapter 7, when I said that there was something unique about Egoic Interpretation? Egoic Interpretation is unique because you can go back in time and change the value of an Egoic Interpretation, and it immediately changes the Being that you are in the present moment and into the future. You can't go back in time and change your Inputs from thirty years ago. If you could do this with Physical Inputs, I know I would definitely not have eaten all the fast food I did as a teenager. However, you can literally do this with your Egoic Interpretations of thirty years ago and change your future in this moment by simply changing an Egoic Interpretation of the past. Let's do it.

EGOIC INTERPRETATION EXERCISE SIX

Egoic Interpretation for any past event can be changed at any time. No need to jump in your favorite time machine; just pull a Life Event into your consciousness and give it a good check-in. See if the Egoic Interpretation that you assigned in the past is still the one you want to hold now. If not, what do you need to do to change it? Your Egoic Interpretation is the one variable completely in your control. Let's give it a try right now. I will give you an example, and then you will do one of your own.

I am going to pick a Life Event that I haven't consciously thought about for many years, but I know the Egoic Interpretation is a negative one that is still with me because, as I remember it now, it feels negative. I was fourteen years old and in the high school weight room. I was a "late bloomer," and while most of my peers had, I had barely, if at all, started puberty. I was lifting weights to try to get in shape for basketball, and I had been lifting weights five times per week for a few months. On this particular day, some girls from the cross-country team were also in the weight room. I was on the bench press, and I had eighty-five pounds on the bar, and this was all I could lift for five repetitions. For reference, I had friends my age who could lift 185 pounds for five repetitions easily.

One of the girls from the cross-country team asked if she could work-in on the bench press with us. She proceeded to add ten more pounds to the bench press bar and do her five repetitions. I then had to remove the ten pounds before I could do my next set of bench press. Needless to say, this was traumatic to my ego. That event instilled in me that I was physically weak and left a negative Egoic Interpretation I have carried for years.

Now, I have pulled this Life Event into my consciousness, and I realize that I was a fourteen-year-old boy who had not gone through puberty. It was not a lack of effort or will on my part and was completely out of my control. I had no reason to feel bad, but as that fourteen-year-old boy in that moment, I was humiliated. However, as a forty-five-year-old man, I have a different perspective and can change the Egoic Interpretation of that Life Event in this moment, like I just have. Now, this change cascades forward to other Egoic Interpretations I am carrying regarding other Life Events where I thought of myself as physically weak. I hope you see how it can ripple throughout your past into your present and change your future.

It is time for you to change an Egoic Interpretation of a past Life Event. What will it be? Transport yourself back to the Life Event just as I did above. See it through the lens of who you are now. Make the change and feel it cascade forward.

HOW TO WORK WITH OTHERS USING THE BEING EQUATION

As I have mentioned in numerous places throughout this book, the assistance and support of others can be invaluable in helping you dig into the Being Equation. In fact, it can be useful to find another person or a small group of people that you trust and go through these exercises together. I would recommend you do the exercises individually before the gathering and then meet weekly or monthly and work through one variable of the Being Equation each session. The insights you gain through this type of group work can be profound, but it has to be done with other Beings that you trust. You have to be able to express your true self for this to work. Do not take this point lightly.

In giving direction on how to support and work with others in exploring the Being Equation, it is useful to think in terms of being an archeologist or a sculptor.

I view an archeologist as someone who looks for things that have been forgotten, lost, buried, or hidden. Once an archeologist thinks they have found something, they cautiously uncover whatever it is, being extremely careful not to damage the artifact or site in the process. The goal of the archeologist is to uncover the artifact in as close to its original condition as possible.

A sculptor, on the other hand, starts with raw material, like a lump of clay, and forms and shapes it into something new. A sculptor creates and shapes while an archeologist uncovers.

This is how I like to think of interacting with the Being Equation in terms of supporting others and using it myself. As we have touched on before, sometimes others can see things about us that we can't see ourselves. When you help others with the Being Equation, you need to think of yourself as an archeologist. Your role is to ask questions and help them uncover their artifacts that have been forgotten, lost, buried, or hidden for themselves. You can help, but they need to do the work for themselves. How do you do this? With the same care and thoughtfulness that an archeologist takes when at an archeological dig site. Your goal is to help the other person uncover what is there so they can see it and figure out what to do with it. Your tools in this process are love and curiosity. You want to do this with as much care as an archeologist would bring.

It is important to realize that you are only trying to uncover what is there. You are not trying to plant a fifteenth century Ming Dynasty vase on the dig site so they can "discover" it for themselves. Your mission is to simply help them uncover what is already there. You do this by being curious and asking questions that are open-ended. We often get stuck in proverbial ruts, and we get our heads down and keep digging and digging at a site for something that might not be there. Your job is to walk up and say, "Hey, have you ever thought about looking over here?" This has to be done from a place of love. There is often, but not always, a reason that something has been forgotten, lost, buried, or hidden. That reason is often related to a source of emotional pain or trauma. If you are not asking questions from a place of love and support, then maybe you shouldn't be asking the person the questions. And if you have a person who is helping you poke around your archeological site and you don't think they are doing it from a place of love and support, thank them for their help and find a new archeologist to work with.

Which brings us to the sculptor. I believe that you are the sculptor of your own life. You are the one who puts your hands on the clay and starts to shape it into whatever you think it should be. The beautiful thing about clay is that if you don't like what is taking shape or if you decide you want a different design altogether, you can mash it all down and start over.

I have a friend who is a sculptor, and he goes to workshops to learn new styles and techniques from other sculptors. Then he comes home and incorporates what he learns into his own unique style. His style and level of skill have changed and grown over time, but it is always his hands touching his clay. There are as many ways to sculpt as there are sculptors. There is no "right" or "wrong" way to sculpt. The only way to take a lump of clay and not create something is to not touch the lump of clay at all.

When it comes to your own life, your objective is to be both an archeologist and a sculptor. You need to be an archeologist and look at the variables of the Being Equation and uncover everything in your life that has made you the Being you are today. Then, become a sculptor and use the Being Equation to shape yourself into the Being you want to become.

When it comes to others, you need to be a loving archeologist and help them uncover their forgotten, lost, buried, or hidden experiences that have made them the Beings they are. However, you are not a sculptor of someone else's life. Never touch someone else's clay. You can show them the tools and techniques you have used in creating your sculpture and the results you have gotten. You can support and encourage them as they work on their sculpture, but never touch their clay.

No matter how much you love them and want to help, ultimately, it always has to be them touching their own clay. If they look at their sculpture and see that one little place you used your hands to shape and fix (even one little spot), it will always be a reminder that their life is no longer solely their own creation; it starts to become a little bit of yours.

BONUS EXERCISES
LOVE, ACCEPTANCE, AND FORGIVENESS EXERCISE

If you are skeptical about the power of love, try this simple exercise: Think about your memories and feelings around the first few days of "falling in love" with someone. How did you feel? How much energy did you have? Could you stay up all night talking? Did it feel good just to be in the other person's company? Did you find it hard to sleep because you were so excited and full of energy?

Now, think about your memories and feelings around the first few days after breaking up with someone? How did you feel? How much energy did you have? Did you find it hard to be around other people? Did you find it hard to be around yourself? Did you have the energy to do even routine tasks? Did you have to drag yourself out of bed in the morning?

Be gentle with yourself as you answer the questions below as they can touch on some very deep emotional wounds. It could take weeks or months of revisiting these questions before you are able to really move into them.

Take some time to periodically journal about these questions, and allow yourself to be curious and accepting of what emerges for you:

- Do you accept yourself exactly as the person you are now?
- Do you forgive yourself, or do you carry an emotional grudge against yourself?
- Are you still carrying the emotional burden of a decision made years ago by a person you no longer are?
- Do you accept others in your life as the people they are now?
- Do you forgive others, or do you carry an emotional grudge against them?

- What stories in your life do you have that start with the words, *I am ashamed of....*?

EMOTIONS AND FEELINGS EXERCISE

It used to be very hard for me to determine my feelings about a particular Life Event because I was strongly suppressing any feelings that came up. It sounds strange, but I had gotten so "good" at suppressing my feelings that I didn't really feel and could not tell you what my true feelings were related to a particular Life Event. This was because I had become so good at paying attention to the feelings of others.

If you are struggling to identify your feelings, here is a good exercise that can help to clarify your feelings about a Life Event: imagine telling the most important person in your life about the thing or Life Event you are trying to determine your feelings about. Now, think about how it would make you *feel* to tell them about that Life Event? Would it make you happy, embarrassed, sad, angry, shy? Once you have the feeling, next ask the question, *why would I feel that way?*

This exercise can be extremely powerful for exploring feelings around Life Events that you don't like to talk about. I have used this exercise to realize that I often layer an emotion that I reference around an event over the deeper, darker emotion that I do not want to face and feel. This is especially prevalent when deep shame or deep sadness is involved.

As we talked about before, burying or hiding feelings takes a tremendous amount of energy and keeps you from showing up in this world as the vibrant, powerful, Spiritual, and Physical Being you are, and that serves no one. Least of all, you.

RELATIONSHIPS EXERCISE

Here is a great exercise to share positive feelings with those Beings in your life. Take out a sheet of paper and make a list of everyone that has had a positive impact on your life. The list can include relationships as close as your significant other, members of your family, and friends all the way to a teacher or coach from school, the barista at the coffee shop, a coworker from three jobs ago, your dog, or an old roommate. If a name pops up in your head, write it down. Over the next few weeks and months, go through this list and find some way to let each person know that they had a positive impact on your life. Give them a call, send them a letter, write them an email, give them a good belly rub (probably best to only belly rub the four-legged creatures), but do *something* to acknowledge the effect of the relationship on you. I can assure you that you will make their day by reaching out to them.

CONCLUSION

This book started with a question: *what am I meant to do?* I told you how attempting to answer this question had led to many years of depression and darkness for me. I also told you that it was the wrong question, at least to start. The question you must start with is: *who am I?* This book is an exploration and guide towards answering that question. In fact, the Being Equation is the mathematical representation of every living Being on this planet, including you, and exactly who you are in this present moment.

What am I meant to do? This was such a difficult question for me because I had a major misconception about the answer—that there would be one, golden, glowing, shining path that would be *what I was meant to do*, and when I discovered it, the clouds would part, bells and trumpets would sound, and I could live happily ever after just by following the path. The rest of my years would be filled with a sense of purpose and direction as I marched down the path set before me. I would reach the end of my life, and as long as I had stayed on the path of what I was meant to do, I would have a sense that I had lived a good life and fulfilled my purpose.

The truth I have found is that it doesn't work that way. There is no single path out there that represents *what you are meant to do*. There is no path that, if you can just find it, you can follow for the rest of your life and that your life will unfold exactly as it is *meant to*. Because there is no *meant to*. You are a powerful creator, and by learning who you are and living in alignment with who you are as a Being you will create your own path. The path doesn't already exist somewhere, and, one day, you find it. The path is one you *create* as you live each day.

Look—for me this is one of those situations where long-form writing starts to feel clunky. As I was trying to decide how to best describe *what you are meant to do*, I was inspired to write the following poem.

PATHS

I am walking along a well-trodden path
and I come to a fork.
I do not know the entire route of either branch
but I know, in general, where each branch leads.

This is my first time on the path
but many people I know have walked these paths.
They have told me many stories of where each path leads.
I pause and look down one branch of the path,

and then I look down the other and think of all the stories.

I can't decide which branch of the path I should follow
so I stand at the fork for many hours.
I finally hear a little voice and realize it is my Heart speaking.
"I know you don't want to take either path," says Heart.
"You are right," I say, "but I do not know what to do."
"Ask Spirit," Heart says, "Spirit will know what to do."
"Good idea, Heart," I say.

"Spirit, I have a choice between two paths and
I don't know which to choose. Can you help me?" I ask.
"You know many people who have walked each of these paths
and you know where each leads, but neither
    is for you," replies Spirit.
"I know Spirit, but they are both good paths, and
    I should be happy with either."
Besides, I say, "there are no other paths to follow."

"Oh," says Spirit, "I didn't know you could only walk
on a path that has been laid before you.
Do your feet only work if they are placed on a path?"
"No," I reply, "My feet will take me anywhere I ask them."
"Heart, will you go with him as well?" asks Spirit.
"Yes," says Heart, "I will go."

And as I raise my eyes and look around,
I see so many possible paths.
"Thank you, Spirit," I reply, as I leave the well-trodden path
and begin making my own path through
    the land that lies before me.

You are meant to do so many things in your life that there is no single answer to the question, so please stop searching for it. As the Being Equation shows, the Being that you are is constantly changing. As you have new Life Events, change old Egoic Interpretations, and challenge stories and your own First Principles that have been controlling your life for years, whole new possibilities will open before you. As these changes occur, *what you are meant to do* will change, and, as I have said, I believe you are meant to do many different things. For example, I went from a biological technician with the federal government to an entrepreneur and writer. Twenty years ago, I would have never even considered my current reality as a possibility. But as the Being I am today has grown and changed, my reality has changed. I am confident that if you apply the Being Equation to your life, what you consider as possible will change and expand, and you will see the question of what you are meant to do in a whole new light.

What I am ultimately saying is that as you live your life more in alignment with who you are, what you are meant to do will create itself. When you focus your time and energy on the things you find truly important, you are focusing the creative energy of the universe, and you will create the life you are meant to live because your life will be your creation in that moment. What you are meant to do is constantly changing because the Being that you are is constantly changing. You see, there is no single path. You are constantly creating the path before you.

Although we have come to the end of this book, I hope that the adventure is just beginning for you. Your life, who you are, and the most relevant question to you in the known universe come down to five variables. Now that you know those five variables, you not only know exactly who you are at this very moment, you know what controls who you will be in the future.

My hope is that you will keep this book on your shelf and refer to it as you explore and grow in these different areas. There is a lot of information in here, and some of it will land differently with you in a year or two. Think of all the new Life Events that will happen to you, and by then, you will have done some digging and sculpting on your life. Certain concepts that you may have skimmed over initially will resonate with you in a completely different way. Maybe you will share the book with a friend or start a small group where you can work through and discuss the Being Equation and help each other on the adventure of answering the question: *who am I?* Thus, creating the life you want to live.

The choice and power are now in your hands. You can use this as a launching point to explore who you are and shape your life into who you want to be, or you can decide this is a quaint little book, that the author seems nice, but a little crazy, and go back to living your status quo life.

Totally up to you. There is no right or wrong, good or bad decision to be made...actually, that's not true. There is absolutely a right choice to be made! This is your life! Realize that you are a powerful creator and use the Being Equation to create the life that you want to live so that you can look back at the end and say, "Wow, that was one epic ride."

If you take nothing else away from this book, please take this one thing: *a life of purpose is not something you find. It is something you create.*

Go create!

ACKNOWLEDGMENTS

I would like to start by acknowledging that this acknowledgments section is much too insignificant a place to acknowledge the people mentioned below. I am also confident there are people I have failed to acknowledge here that I most certainly would like to. If you happen to be in this category, please accept my sincere apologies and gratitude.

For now, we must start somewhere, so let's begin. First, I acknowledge you, the reader. Without you there would be no need for this book. I appreciate you taking the time and effort to read these words.

Christi, for the gift of your companionship on this adventure of life. For reading and editing this book, for knowing when to give me a nice big hug or a swift kick in the ass. For giving me the time and space to figure out who I am and for not knowing what's coming next and still being excited for the ride. I love you.

Mom, for always loving, supporting, and encouraging me. For telling me, if I didn't come home with skinned-up knees, I wasn't playing hard enough, and for frying trout in a hotel room.

Dad, for walks in nature, time spent fishing, sitting under the stars, sleeping in an old pup tent, and basketball. Although we never discussed writing, I know this love of words came from you.

Dr. Lynn Fichter, for the countless hours spent answering five-point critical thinking questions with no reward for right or wrong but the prize for showing a train of thought. Thank you for teaching me how to think. Yours was the most valuable course of my undergraduate career.

Andrew Bryan, for teaching me to work hard and that the best conversations can happen while sitting on a cooler, enjoying a pack of crackers and soda. Every time I see it, your art never ceases to amaze me.

Larry Kendall, for introducing me to the world of personal growth and development and being a mentor and supporter as I ventured onto this new ground.

Philip McKernan, for looking over the cliff and giving me a push to see what lies beyond. I consider you an *anam cara*, and I do not use those words lightly. Meet you at Margaret's for a pint.

Joshua Sneideman, Shari Moss, Zach Obront, and Dave Rizzotto for early reviews, comments, and words of encouragement with this manuscript. Also, for Cuban cigars, introductions to spirit guides, publishing advice, and long, rambling conversations over red wine. I will leave it up to each of you to figure out who is getting acknowledged for what.

To the Tribe of Gobundace for the support and example of what is possible.

To the men of the FOCO MM or "brain camp" as one person likes to call it. Thank you for the love and support and for not being afraid to show up as who you are.

To Dr. Hans Jenny for *Factors of Soil Formation*.

Elizabeth Gilbert for the encouragement and inspiration. We have yet to meet in person (I sincerely hope we do—you are one of my dream dinner party guests) but your book, *Big Magic*, guided me to make a contract with this idea and grab the tiger by the tail. When I needed you, your voice was in my ear, and your words were in my heart, encouraging me. Thank you.

To the canine, feline, equine and porcine friends that I have been privileged to share time with including, but not limited to: TG, Garfield, Joshua, Sam, Owen, Squeakers, Winston, Oskar, Aspen Annie the Wonder Kitty, Jessi Bean, Jimmie, Ryder, Señor and Miss Piggy Sue. If you find it odd that I am acknowledging these beings, then you really need to spend more time with four legged friends. You will understand.

To my editors, Berit Oskey Coleman and Amanda Woodard, for looking at the stack of Lincoln Logs and having the vision and skill to turn them into something resembling a cabin. Thank you.

Libby Allen and the entire Scribe Team for helping turn the dream of a book into reality.

If you happen to be someone I should have acknowledged and I did not do so, please be so kind as to drop me a note in the mail, and I will add you to the acknowledgments when the tenth anniversary edition of this book is printed to celebrate the milestone of selling ten million copies worldwide...a boy can dream.

Love, Erik

ABOUT THE AUTHOR

ERIK HARDY lives in a horse barn with his wife, five horses, a border collie, and a pot-bellied pig named Miss Piggy Sue. He writes and works from his Airstream, ACE Gratitude.

Erik worked as a gardener, a medical IT consultant, a bank teller, an ecologist, and a real estate broker, moving from one career to another without any sense of purpose or direction before he finally started asking the right question.

By discovering who he really is and living in alignment with his true self, he has found authentic joy as an entrepreneur, writer, and creator, living his life on purpose and turning his dreams into his reality. He wrote this book to help you do the same.

Learn more at erikhardy.com.

CPSIA information can be obtained
at www.ICGtesting.com
Printed in the USA
BVHW071826291021
620255BV00003B/14